FROM STILL TO MOTION

MOTION

Editing DSLR Video with **Final Cut Pro X**

RICHARD HARRINGTON > **ABBA SHAPIRO** > **ROBBIE CARMAN**

From Still to Motion
Editing DSLR Video with Final Cut Pro X

Richard Harrington, Abba Shapiro, and Robbie Carman

Peachpit Press
1249 Eighth Street
Berkeley, CA 94710
(510) 524-2178
Fax: (510) 524-2221

Find us on the Web at www.peachpit.com
To report errors, please send a note to errata@peachpit.com
Peachpit is a division of Pearson Education

Senior Editor: Karyn Johnson
Copy Editor: Anne Marie Walker
Production Editor: Cory Borman
Composition: Kim Scott, Bumpy Design
Proofreader: Elizabeth Welch
Indexer: Valerie Perry
Interior Design: Mimi Heft, with Kim Scott
Cover Design: Mimi Heft
Cover Photograph: Lisa Robinson, Bess Johnson, and Richard Harrington
Cover Model: Irene Magafan

ISBN-13: 978-0-321-81125-7
ISBN-10:   0-321-81125-9

9 8 7 6 5 4 3 2 1

Printed and bound in the United States of America

Acknowledgments

Adorama
Apple
Scott Bourne
Kevin Bradley
Canon
John and Marcia Carman
Scott Cowlin
Sam Crawford
Creative COW
Mark Fuccio
Mimi Heft

Bess Johnson
Karyn Johnson
Dave Joyce
Ben Kozuch
Vincent Laforet
Lynda.com
John Lytle
Nikon
Jason Osder
Cheryl Ottenritter
Staff of Otthouse Audio

Christopher Phrommayon
Garrett O'Brien
Staff of RHED Pixel
Lisa Robinson
Jeff Snyder
Anne Marie Walker
Mark Weiser
Aaron Wold
John Woody
Zacuto

Contents

Introduction

When we wrote the first book in this series—*From Still to Motion: A photographer's guide to creating video with your DSLR*—our intent was to explore the entire creative process from preproduction through postproduction. The feedback on that book has been overwhelmingly positive, as have your requests for more details and workflows.

We're glad to bring you the next book in this series—*From Still to Motion: Editing DSLR Video with Final Cut Pro X*—to make the editing and delivery processes easier. Final Cut Pro X offers a whole new way to edit, with an ease of use that opens the door for millions of new users. Up until now, editing DSLR video has been anything but easy—syncing sound, transcoding footage, fixing rolling shutter—but the "look" made it all worthwhile.

We wrote this targeted guide on editing DSLR video with Final Cut Pro X to help you generate results immediately. We wanted to strip away the many options and overly complex choices, and just focus on what a DSLR video shooter needs to become an editor. This book is for users of all levels who want to learn how to:

> Import, analyze, and organize your footage and media

> Set up your projects correctly for any DSLR camera

> Fix common problems like exposure, rolling shutter, and shaky video

> Implement essential and advanced editing techniques

> Work with synchronized sound and create compelling audio mixes

> Correct color and exposure problems with your clips

> Publish and share your productions to the Web and mobile devices

Meet the Cast

This book is truly a team effort, much like the video production process. Because video is a multifaceted undertaking, we've come together to guide you through the process of creating a professional video using Final Cut Pro X.

The Authors

Meet the three authors behind this book. We've collaborated on each chapter to bring you the best of our collective knowledge.

RICHARD HARRINGTON

Richard Harrington is a director/producer with national PSAs and Ciné award-winning productions. He is also a certified instructor for Apple and Adobe, and an expert in motion graphic design and digital video. He is a regular contributor to Creative COW, *Photoshop User* magazine, and numerous industry blogs. He also owns the visual communications company RHED Pixel (www.rhedpixel.com) in Washington, D.C. Rich is a member of the National Association of Photoshop Professionals Instructor Dream Team, manages conferences for the National Association of Broadcasters, and has written and co-written a number of books, including *Understanding Adobe Photoshop* (Peachpit, 2010), *Photoshop for Video* (Peachpit, 2010), and *Video Made on a Mac* (Peachpit, 2009). You can contact Rich at:

> www.linkedin.com/in/richardharrington

> www.rhedpixel.com

> www.richardharringtonblog.com

> www.3exposure.com

> www.twitter.com/rhedpixel

ABBA SHAPIRO

Abba Shapiro is a lead instructor for Apple's Pro Video Apps certified training program, certifying other instructors since the program's inception. He is also co-author of the advanced editing tips and tricks book, *Final Cut Studio on the Spot* (Focal Press, 2007), with Richard Harrington and Robbie Carman.

Abba is an award-winning writer/producer/director with over 25 years experience in video and film production. He has done work for a wide range of commercial, corporate, and federal clients, including USA Today, The Associated Press, NASA, Univision, and the Department of Defense.

In addition to production, Abba has been teaching in the Washington, D.C. area and around the planet since the mid 1980s. He teaches a variety of broadcast editing tools, scriptwriting, Photoshop for video, and producing and production workshops at venues such as NAB, IBC, Macworld, Government Video Expo, and New York Post Production World. You can contact Abba at:

> www.shapirovideo.com

> www.linkedin.com/pub/abba-shapiro/1/264/964

ROBBIE CARMAN

Robbie Carman is a professional colorist who works on broadcast television series and independent films. He's part of the first generation of certified Apple Final Cut Pro instructors and Color. Robbie co-wrote *Final Cut Pro Workflows* (Focal Press, 2007) with Jason Osder as well as *Final Cut Studio on the Spot* (Focal Press, 2007) and *Video Made on a Mac* (Peachpit, 2009) with Richard Harrington and Abba Shapiro. Robbie speaks internationally at conferences, such as the National Association of Broadcasters (NAB) and the International Broadcasting Convention (IBC). Robbie is the co-owner of Amigo Media (www.amigomediallc.com), a boutique postproduction company located in Washington, D.C. You can contact Robbie at:

> www.linkedin.com/in/robbiecarman

> www.amigomediallc.com

> www.robbiecarman.net

> www.twitter.com/robbiecarman

Documentary Photographer

Although there are many photos in the book, we had one principal photographer who helped us document the experience.

LISA ROBINSON

Lisa Robinson began her studies of photography in 1999 and immediately knew it would be a lifelong career. She began work as a print technician for Kodak and took any assistant jobs available while completing college. In 2005 she graduated Magna Cum Laude in Applied Media Arts & Photography from Edinboro University and started work with Apple, Inc. Her work with Apple put her in touch with the vast array of technology associated with digital photography and further cultivated her passion for beautiful images. Together with Ian Robinson, she founded SoftBox

Media in 2006 and began photographing weddings in the Washington, D.C. area and beyond. In 2008 she became a member of The Professional Photographers of America. Recently, Lisa's work has earned SoftBox Media the Bride's Choice Award 2010 from WeddingWire.com and TheKnot.com's Best of Weddings 2010 pick for photography in the D.C. metro area.

Music

We are grateful to Aaron Wold and the band Minimus the Poet for sharing their music and story with us. Please explore the band's website to hear more of their music.

MINIMUS THE POET

Minimus the Poet began as a solo project. The brainchild of Aaron Wold, a Baltimore transplant, has blossomed into an indie/folk quintet, and the band is making its mark on the Charm City scene.

Wold composed, performed, recorded, and produced the album *E S O*, which was released independently in 2009. The album received high praise from local media, and a small cult following began to develop. Due to increasing demand for live performances from

Minimus the Poet
Married In The Mud

the fan base, Wold recruited some of the area's most talented musicians to lend their skills, and they took to the stage. Since their first live, full-band appearance, Minimus the Poet has performed at nearly every major venue in the Baltimore area, branching out into Western Maryland, Pennsylvania, and surrounding cities. In 2010, a sophomore release followed, titled *Married in the Mud*. The EP features five original tracks co-written and performed by the band.

Minimus the Poet has been described as "folk rock," and "experimental folk," mostly in response to the wide range of instrumentation evident on its recordings and performances. David Engwall rotates from banjo to mandolin to electric guitar. Melissa Thompson plays piano, accordion, and percussion. Matt Flanders plays bass and percussion. Wold plays both acoustic and electric guitar, and—most notably—the theremin. A wide range of percussive instruments and vocals garnish nearly every song in the band's repertoire.

Wold cites a wide range of musical artists as being influential—everything from 90s rock, including Gin Blossoms, Silverchair, and Radiohead, to contemporary bluegrass artists like Chris Thile. He is also inspired by classical thereminists, such as Clara Rockmore and iconic country artists Patsy Cline and Elvis Presley, and can be quoted saying, "It took a heavy dose of punk rock to get over my stage fright. I suppose I have Bad Religion to thank for that."

Minimus the Poet is currently working on a third studio release. Visit www.minimusthepoet.com for more music, videos, and information.

About the Lesson Files

In your hands is a book, but there are files that accompany these lessons. Here's how to download them.

1. Visit www.peachpit.com/register to register your book.
2. Log in or create a new account at Peachpit.com.
3. Enter this book's ISBN number: 0321811259.
4. You will be given access to this book's download files.

You'll find different items included in the download:

> The actual footage shot in this project
> A video overview of Final Cut Pro X
> Additional resources on color correction and grading

What You Need

Welcome to a high-tech world. You won't need the latest and greatest, but we do have some strong recommendations. To complete the exercises in this book, you'll need:

> Mac computer with an Intel Core 2 Duo processor or better.
> Final Cut Pro X (Compressor also recommend).
> 2 GB of RAM (4 GB of RAM recommended).
> OpenCL-capable graphics card.
> 256 MB of VRAM.
> Display with 1280x768 resolution or higher.
> OS X v10.6.8 or later.
> A high-speed hard drive with a FireWire or SATA connection for editing video files. Internal laptop or computer drives can work, but a performance drive (RAID) is highly recommended.

CHAPTER 1

Shooting with Editing in Mind

Editing is the process of assembling the acquired footage to tell a story. For this to successfully occur, you'll need footage that matches the technical and artistic needs of your project.

Your editing stage actually begins when you fire your first shot on your DSLR camera. Once you've started gathering footage, the ideal project settings for video editing quickly get locked in. As such, we think it's important to always double-check that what's being shot is what you actually want to acquire.

In addition, it's important to ensure that you are getting great audio. It's very easy to overlook audio in the middle of focusing and composing shots. But without clear sound, you often don't have a story (or an audience).

Let's briefly review the most important choices you'll make during production that will impact your postproduction experience.

Camera Settings

Press the menu button on any DSLR camera, and you'll literally see page after page of choices. With hundreds of options, it's pretty easy to screw things up. The good news is that when it comes to video, you only have a few choices to make. Let's quickly review some of the essential camera settings and discuss their overlap with editing.

Frame Size (Resolution)

When shooting stills on a DSLR camera, you'll find different megapixel counts that describe the dimensions of the photos taken. For example, the Canon 7D shoots an 18 megapixel image with dimensions of 5134 x 3456. The Nikon D7000 captures a 16.1 megapixel image with dimensions of 4928 x 3264. These numbers define the resolution and size of the image at 100 percent, or full resolution.

When shooting video, however, both cameras offer the same choices. Here are the two HD standards you'll encounter:

> 1920 x 1080 (known as full HD)

> 1280 x 720 (known as 720p HD)

Although some cameras only offer one of these two frame sizes, both are acceptable for modern HD video production. These standards are essential so that video cameras, software, and displays can all work together. Make sure that you discuss project requirements with the client or producer to ensure that the footage acquired matches the needs of the project.

If the choice is up to you, like most editors, you should favor the 1080 flavor for its larger image. However, if storage space during capture or editing is at a premium, the 720 frame size offers much smaller files. Many cameras also offer faster frame rates for 720 for motion effects or overcranking.

Frame Rate

Depending on the manufacturer, you'll find a wide range of frame rates offered. These choices are meant to create compatibility with the many broadcast standards used around the world.

Your DSLR likely supports some (or all) of these frame rates (measured in frames per second):

> **60 fps (59.94 fps).** A common frame rate for 720p HD used in the United States and other NTSC-based countries.

> **50 fps.** A common frame rate for 720p HD used in Europe and other PAL-based countries.

1920 x 1080 (full HD)

1280 x 720 (720p HD)

> **30 fps (really 29.97 fps).** The most common frame rate for broadcast in the United States and other NTSC-based countries.

> **25 fps.** The common frame rate of video used in Europe and additional markets around the world that are based on the PAL standard.

> **24 fps (23.98 or 23.976 fps).** A rate that closely matches that of film.

It is important that you minimize mixing frame rates in a project because it can lead to extra rendering time and jerky-looking footage. Choosing a frame rate is often dictated by what you intend to do with the footage:

> If you want a motion-picture film look, 24 fps is very popular. This rate works well for Web, DVD, and Blu-ray distribution.

> If you are shooting footage that's destined for traditional broadcasting, 25 fps for PAL and 30 (29.97) fps for NTSC is a common choice.

> If you want to achieve motion effects (such as slow motion), overcranking is the way to go. In this case the camera records at a higher frame rate, and you can stretch the clip in postproduction to make smoother slow-motion effects.

Codec

The word *codec* is really a portmanteau (the combining of two words to make a new word). *Compressor + decompressor = codec*. The compressor is in the camera (which shrinks the original footage to fit on the memory card). When you play back a clip or transfer it to a computer, the decompressor (installed as a system extension) expands the data into a video signal.

DON'T SEE A FRAME RATE?
If you can't find a desired frame rate, you might have to tweak the camera settings. Some cameras offer a choice to switch between NTSC and PAL modes. This can affect the available frame rates and sometimes even frame sizes.

Frame Rate Confusion

The more you work in postproduction, the more frame rate choices you'll discover. Many more options are available when you edit than a DSLR camera can shoot. Let's review what the numbers mean.

A technical notation such as 1080p24 describes a format's frame size (resolution), scanning method (interlaced or progressive), and frame rate. In the notation 1080p24:

> The number 1080 means that the format has a vertical resolution of 1080 pixels.

> The p indicates a progressive (p) format. Note that all DSLR video cameras shoot progressive formats for HD video.

> The ending digits specify the frame rate or field rate of the format (which is where most people get confused).

DSLR cameras only capture frames. When you choose from 24, 25, 30, or 60 fps in the menu, you truly are recording that many frames per second. Depending on your camera's firmware, modes like 30 and 60 are most likely being recorded using the fractional values of 29.97 and 59.94.

The real confusion occurs with interlaced video (which many other HD cameras shoot). Often, DSLR video files are mixed with video from other camera types, so the chance for confusion is very likely. Additionally, because most broadcast television is sent in an interlaced format, there is a chance that your DSLR footage may play back on an interlaced display.

Interlaced scanning uses a method where half of the image loads first, and then the other half follows. Each line is scanned very quickly: For example, most broadcast television in the United States has a frame rate of 29.97 frames per second, so each field is scanned in at 1/59.94 of a second. Adding both fields together produces one complete frame. There are two fields in every frame (one even and one odd) on an interlaced TV set. So think of 30 frames a second as 60 even and odd fields.

Table 1.1 shows some common formats in shorthand that you'll encounter on video cameras and in nonlinear editing systems.

Table 1.1 Shorthand Notations for Video Formats

SHORTHAND	FRAME SIZE	SCANNING METHOD	FRAME RATE
1080i60	1920 x 1080	Interlaced	30 fps (29.97 fps)
1080i50	1920 x 1080	Interlaced	25 fps
1080p60	1920 x 1080	Progressive	60 fps (59.94 fps)
1080p50	1920 x 1080	Progressive	50 fps
1080p24	1920 x 1080	Progressive	24 fps (23.98 fps)
720p60	1280 x 720	Progressive	60 fps (59.94 fps)
720p50	1280 x 720	Progressive	50 fps
720p24	1280 x 720	Progressive	24 fps (23.98 fps)

QUALITY MODE
Some cameras offer different quality modes when shooting video. Without question, choose the High-quality mode because video footage on a DSLR is heavily compressed when it gets to the memory card.

When shooting DSLR video, the codec choice is typically made for you by the camera. Not all formats in DSLR cameras are supported by Final Cut Pro X. It's a good idea to check the list of supported formats at www.apple.com/finalcutpro/specs. Just scroll to the section called Supported Formats and I/O.

The three common formats that will likely work include:

> **H.264.** The H.264/MPEG-4 Part 10 format is one of the most commonly used video formats on the market. It is used for both acquisition and delivery. Cameras like the Canon 5D Mark II and 7D as well as the Nikon D7000 use this format.

> **AVCHD.** The AVCHD (Advanced Video Coding High Definition) format is owned jointly by Sony and Panasonic. You'll find it in use on cameras such as the Panasonic Lumix GH2.

> **Motion JPEG.** The Motion JPEG or Photo JPEG format is an older format that was first adopted in early Nikon cameras that shot video. This format is not as broadly supported by video editing tools and has subsequently been dropped in favor of H.264.

The Exposure Triangle

Working with video footage in Final Cut Pro X is a lot easier when you have a proper exposure. Because video footage is fairly compressed, you don't have as much latitude during grading to adjust exposure. We're firm believers in shooting it right and editing less.

There are three components to getting a properly exposed shot: aperture, shutter speed, and ISO.

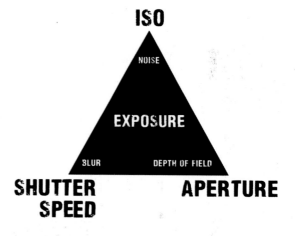

THIS EXPOSURE IS ALMOST RIGHT
When it comes to shooting DSLR footage, it's best to lean to the side of properly exposed or slightly underexposed. It's easier to lighten footage that's a little too dark than to try to restore footage that's overblown. Be sure to watch those highlights (especially the sky).

Aperture

The aperture is typically expressed as the *f*-stop or relative aperture. Each one-stop increment lets in half the light gathering area of the previous one. Using a wide aperture is useful for low-light shooting; it also produces the shallow depth of field or bokeh effect that is a popular aesthetic reason to shoot DSLR video.

Shutter Speed

The shutter speed is another way of controlling how long the camera shutter is open, which further impacts the amount of light on the sensor. When shooting video, however, you'll typically choose options like 1/45, 1/50, or 1/60. It's important to use these speeds for natural-looking motion.

To get a true filmic image, you need to use the optimum shutter angle to accompany the frame rate. Here is a simple formula that you can use to identify the ideal shutter speed: **one second / (frame rate x 2)**.

For example, when you're shooting 24 fps, you would set your camera to use 1/48 of a second exposure time. If you're shooting at 30 fps, you would use 1/60 of a second. If the exact matching rate is not available, choose the closest match. Adhering to this rule ensures that the motion blur created by the camera looks natural. Although you can manipulate shutter speed for purposes of stylizing footage or to compensate for extreme lighting challenges, we recommend you try to stick to this basic formula.

ISO

The ISO settings on your camera match settings established by the International Organization for Standardization. You can adjust this setting to modify how sensitive the camera sensor is to light. Using a lower ISO is important when shooting under bright conditions. If you're shooting under low light, you may need to bump up the ISO. As you start to get past ISO 800, more noise will become apparent in the image. When we get over ISO 1600, we'll change the shutter speed to 1/30 to let in more light.

READ MORE ABOUT PRODUCTION

If you want to fully explore our approach to DSLR production, be sure to pick up a copy of *From Still to Motion: A Photographer's Guide to Creating Video with Your DSLR* (Peachpit, 2010).

ISO AS LOW AS IT GOES?

If you're shooting outdoors under bright lighting, you might run out of ISO. To combat this problem, you can use a neutral density (ND) filter or a matte box to further reduce the amount of light going through the lens and onto your camera's sensor.

Capturing Great Audio

Many are drawn to shooting with DSLR cameras because of the great look they produce, but many are turned off by their audio-capture capabilities. It turns out that the camera manufacturers have pretty much skimped when it comes to audio.

The microphone quality of DSLR cameras falls well below the typical cell phone. Good audio is a key component of a successful video, so make sure that you carefully consider your audio when you're capturing video. One benefit of the on-camera mic is that it is unusually good at picking up your grunts of frustration when your shot is not working.

Internal Microphone

The microphone built into your DSLR camera is worthless for all but the most basic tasks. The microphone is low quality and too close to the lens and camera mechanisms (hence prone to picking up unwanted noise). You can use this microphone for a syncing source, and that's about it.

On-camera Microphone

Strongly consider using an external, shotgun-style microphone that attaches to the hot shoe of your camera. You can plug these microphones into the microphone port on your camera. They are great at picking up better audio and make a cleaner source for reference audio when syncing. They're also good enough to use for background audio and environmental sound for b-roll.

MONITOR ALWAYS

If you aren't listening to your audio while it records, you're taking a great risk. You can miss common audio issues like overmodulation or electrical interference. We strongly recommend wearing over-the-ear headphones while recording. Many DSLR cameras won't let you listen during recording (and even lack a headphone port). This is another reason to record to an external device.

Pre-amps

If you want to use professional microphones with your DSLR camera, you can utilize an audio interface (such as one made by juicedLink or BeachTek). These devices let you connect up to two audio inputs to a DSLR camera.

Features to consider include:

> **Phantom power.** Some models offer phantom power to provide the required charge for certain microphones.

> **Disable Automatic Gain Control (AGC).** Many DSLR cameras use Automatic Gain Control to adjust audio levels on the fly. This can lead to very noisy audio as well as unwanted rapid changes. AGC is dangerous, because if the scene is quiet, the camera boosts the mic's sensitivity, and you tend to pick up unwanted ambience noise, such as air conditioners and street noise.

Dual-System Sound

The most popular approach for DSLR cameras is the same used by film, a dual-system approach. This means that you have two "systems" for recording: one for audio and the other for video. This method is popular because it lets the camera move in an untethered manner without the need for expensive wireless technology. These recorders also tend to offer visible meters, professional connection options, and monitoring via headphones.

Several different recorders are on the market. Most record to either removable media like an SD card or to an internal drive or flash memory. Be sure to avoid the more heavily compressed options (such as MP3). Final Cut Pro X is happiest with an AIFF or WAV file that's recorded at 48 kHz and 16 bit.

Many manufacturers of digital audio recorders exist, but we've had great experiences with the following:

> H4N and H2 from Zoom (www.zoom.co.jp)

> 7 Series family from Sound Devices (www.sounddevices.com)

> DR and HD series from Tascam (www.tascam.com)

▲ Devices like the Zoom H4N assist in recording higher-quality audio that can be synced with a DSLR camera.

DSLR Syncing

If you use a dual-system sound approach, using a slate becomes an essential item. The slate serves two real purposes. First, it gives you a visual reference on the clip of important details for the project. If you hold the slate up before rolling, you can actually see these thumbnails when browsing clips in your project.

Second, a slate offers an audio and visual cue for lining up your video clip with the reference sound. Final Cut Pro X has its own tools for syncing sound, and others are on the market as well. We'll explore this workflow in Chapter 6, "Syncing Footage."

Here are a few tips for shooting sync sound to make editing video and audio easier:

> **Use a clapboard.** There's a reason film productions use a clapboard. When picture and sound are recorded to two different systems, a clapboard makes it easy to synchronize, because it creates a visual and audio cue point. A traditional dry-erase slate will run you about $40–$80. A good place to pick one up is at www.filmtools.com.

> **Use a slate application.** Several applications exist for smart phones and tablet computers that allow you to load information about the production. They can also generate a countdown slate and sync point. One of our favorite features is the ability to geotag your location so you can find a shoot location in the future. Two apps that we use are DSLR Slate (www.lastshotapps.com) and MovieSlate (www.pureblendsoftware.com). Both apps will run on any iOS device. If you use an Android OS, we recommend checking out SL DigiSlate (apps.mech-nology.com).

> **Use your hands.** A clapboard is nice to have, but it often gets forgotten or misplaced on set. In a pinch you can make your own visual and audio reference sync points. The easiest way to do this is simply by clapping your hands and recording the sound to video and audio. Plus, you can even count up to ten takes. If you exceed ten takes, do not take off your shoes; just hold up your fingers twice.

CHAPTER 2

Backing Up Your Data

You've shot the footage you needed;

now what? You're probably eager to jump right in and start editing, and we understand that, but you should first complete a few important tasks that shouldn't be overlooked. These tasks include backing up footage that you shot and transferring it from the camera memory card to field storage and finally to media or editing storage.

We know that backup and data integrity are not the sexiest of subjects, but they're perhaps the most important part of any tapeless workflow, including when working with DSLR footage. After all, you may have shot some beautiful footage, but that beautiful footage won't do you any good if you lose it between production and post. In this chapter we'll dive right in and take a look at backing up and archiving.

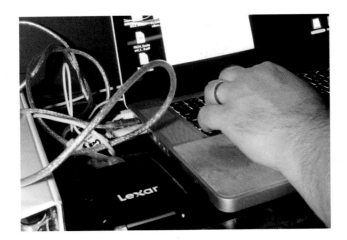

Direct to Edit or Back Up First?

You're really proud of the footage you just shot on your DSLR, and you're ready to jump right in and start editing (and Final Cut Pro X will allow you to do this). Slow down! We strongly urge you to think about backing up your footage prior to editing. When you back up footage, you ensure that if anything should go wrong later in the postproduction pipeline, you'll be able to return to your backup and gain access to the original footage once again.

Backup Workflow

OK, we'll admit there are many different backup workflows, but we'd like to suggest an overall backup workflow that we use all the time. In subsequent sections, we'll break down the following workflow steps into more detail.

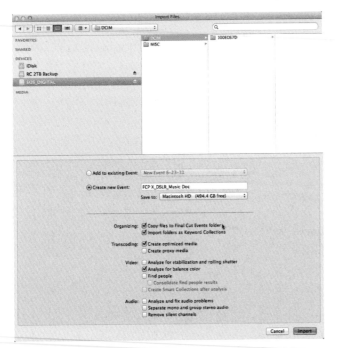

▲ Final Cut Pro X can import media directly from a memory card; however, we suggest you first back up memory cards and then import media from those backups.

1. **Mount memory cards on a portable machine.** Using a memory card reader or a USB cable between your computer and camera, mount a memory card to gain access to footage contained on that card.

2. **Transfer footage to field drives.** After mounting cards to a portable computer, transfer that footage and data to a portable drive (or better yet, multiple portable drives). If a drives fails (when it fails), you'll have a backup. Don't put off backing up your media. You can do this immediately by copying the contents of a memory card as folders and files to a portable drive or by creating a disk image (.dmg).

3. **Transfer field drives to media (edit) storage.** When you get back to your studio, transfer media from your field drives to proper media or edit-caliber storage.

4. **Archive data.** Typically, after transferring media from field storage, archive it to a long-term storage medium. This can be a RAID-protected disk drive (see the section "RAID" later in this chapter) or a long-term solution like Blu-ray Disc.

Transferring Media

The first step in a backup workflow is transferring media from a camera memory card to another storage device, such as a portable hard drive. This process is essential for two reasons: being able to use camera memory cards again and maintaining data integrity. In this section we'll explain the essentials of transferring media in the field.

Selecting a Computer

When you're out in the field, laptops are your friends. These portable computers are great because they allow you to easily interface with camera memory cards (through a card reader or directly by attaching to a camera), as well as portable hard drives. Essentially, each laptop that you bring into the field serves as an offloading station, allowing you to quickly mount, back up, and cycle camera memory cards while you're in the field. However, you should consider a few details when selecting a portable machine for use in the field:

> **No need for latest and greatest.** Because you'll mainly be using your portable machine for transferring footage from memory cards to portable storage, in most cases there is no overwhelming need for the latest and greatest portable machine. We've found that using machines that are two, three, or even four years old work just fine. Just make sure that the laptop can run the applications you'll need to use in the field. Also, you might want to update to a larger internal hard drive to ease your workflow if you are not using a portable backup drive.

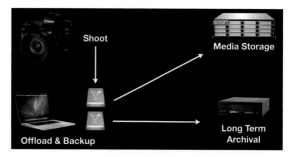

▲ Our suggested backup workflow is to shoot and then back up memory card contents to two, portable field-storage drives. Back at the studio, transfer that media to an edit or media drive, and then archive the contents of the portable drives to long-term storage like Blu-ray or LTO (Linear Tape Open).

▲ Portable computers can serve as offloading stations in the field.

FAST MEMORY CARDS MEAN FAST TRANSFER
Although the fastest SD and CF cards are often not needed for DSLR video, they do offer one big benefit: They make transferring footage much faster when paired with a fast card reader. We recommend SDHC Class 10 or UDMA rated cards. When you plug those into a fast port (like FireWire 800 or Thunderbolt), you'll speed through the transfer.

> **Connectivity.** Although you don't need the latest and greatest computer, it does help to have connectivity that will work for what you're trying to do. USB 2.0, FireWire 400 or 800, or an ExpressCard slot are all good things to have for fast data transfer.

> **Software.** Make sure you have Final Cut Pro X and other applications that you'll use back in the studio on your portable machine if possible. Keep in mind that if your portable machine is too old, you might not be able to run the latest OS and other apps. Having the essential apps on the field laptop makes it possible to quickly check technical issues as well as create quick edits so you can check for continuity (and other issues) in the footage you've shot.

Selecting a Portable Drive

When you're out in the field, your portable computer becomes your transfer or offloading station. Although you can transfer material directly to the internal drive of a portable machine, drives in those machines are typically pretty small. Also, when you get back to your studio, if media is located on the internal drive of your portable machine, it can make transferring footage to edit-grade storage cumbersome. To resolve these issues, it is best to use portable media drives. They are inexpensive and can attach to whatever computer you are using in the field and during your edit for easy transfer.

No doubt you've used a portable hard drive before. Here are a couple of features to look for when choosing a portable drive:

> **Bus power.** You don't want to have to deal with extra power adapters while in the field. Be sure to select drives that can be bus powered so they can use the laptop's power and not need a separate plug.

> **Speed.** Portable field drives that use mechanical drive units usually come in one of two speeds: 5400 or 7200 rpm. Select the faster speed to facilitate rapid transfer of camera memory cards.

▲ Portable drives, like the one shown here, are great for transferring footage from memory cards through a portable computer.

 WHERE TO GET PORTABLE DRIVES?
Although there are a plethora of places to get portable drives, one of our favorite vendors is Other World Computing (www.macsales.com). It offers portable solutions in a variety of configurations. Be sure to check it out.

> **Connectivity.** Be sure to select a drive with varied connectivity. FireWire 400 and 800 or USB 2.0 are natively supported for portable drive units. USB 3.0 as well as eSATA are good choices for connectivity (but require additional hardware).

> **Go SSD.** Solid State Drives (SSDs) are becoming more common and are the future of data storage. Because there are no moving parts in an SSD drive, the chances of failure are low and the drive is generally much faster than its mechanical cousins. The downside of these drives is that they don't have a very large capacity. As of this writing, 512 GB is about as big as you can find. And with the latest and greatest comes an increase in price. Good SSD drives can cost quite a bit more compared to traditional portable hard drives.

Using a Card Reader

To transfer and back up media in the field, you'll need a card reader. Now you might be thinking, why do I need a card reader? I can just use a USB cable between my camera and laptop in the field. Although this is generally true, you don't want to tie up your camera to transfer footage. Also, you don't want to risk damaging your camera through wear and tear on a mini-USB connection that's directly attached to the main circuitry of your camera.

You might also be thinking that your computer or laptop has a built-in memory card reader. Most of the time, those built-in readers (always the case on Macs) are actually only SD card readers, which won't do you any good if you shoot with Compact Flash cards. So having a card reader is vital to facilitate the backup of memory cards while in the field. The issue you'll probably have to debate most when choosing a card reader is its connection type—whether it is FireWire (400 and 800), USB (1, 2, 3), or ExpressCard.

With any of these connection types, you'll still have a lot of readers to choose from. Here are some specific features to look for in a card reader:

> **Bus power.** Look for a reader that is bus powered, which allows for the card reader to operate without additional external power. It can run simply by using the connection bus to your computer, like FireWire or USB.

> **Speed.** Transferring footage quickly largely depends on card speed, but a slow card reader can handicap even a fast card. We've found when transferring large video files that FireWire 800 card readers and ExpressCard adapters are the best bets.

> **Multiple slots.** Many card readers offer two or even four slots, which are handy for loading additional cards. Backing up often happens quickly while in the field; being able to load up a few cards and walk away from your computer lets you get back to shooting quickly.

▲ Portable card readers allow you to quickly mount DSLR memory cards and transfer them to portable storage through a portable computer.

Offloading Cards as Folders and Files to a Portable Drive

When you're in the field, the quickest and easiest way to back up your camera memory cards is to simply copy all of the folders and files on a card to a directory (folder) on a portable field hard drive. However, if you're going to copy the contents of a camera memory card to a new folder like this, you need to keep two considerations in mind:

> **Copy all files and folders.** You need to make sure when you're copying the contents of a memory card that you copy all of the folders and files off the original memory card. You could just copy the video files (usually located in a DCIM folder), but this wouldn't be a complete backup of the original memory card. In some cases, if you only

back up the DCIM folder, you may not even be able to read your backup data, because critical files and metadata may be missing.

> **Mounting as original card.** Unlike creating a disk image (which we'll talk about next), when you copy folders and files from a memory card to a portable field drive, you won't be able to mount that data like the original camera memory card.

TRY SHOTPUT PRO

One of the handiest applications we've found for offloading footage in the field is called ShotPut Pro by Imagine Products. It allows you to back up in multiple locations, perform Checksum operations, and automate the transfer process. Check it out at www.imagineproducts.com.

Creating Disk Images on a Portable Drive

One of the best ways to back up footage shot on your DSLR is to create a self-contained file called a disk image. A *disk image* is an exact duplicate of the original camera memory card. Disk images offer two major benefits over simply offloading files on cards to a portable drive while in the field:

> **File protection.** When you create a disk image, all files are stored in a .dmg file. One advantage is that it makes it more difficult to accidentally modify individual files and folders. This anti-tampering is important because editorial applications like Final Cut Pro X may not be able to read incomplete folder and file structures from tapeless media sources, such as those from a DSLR.

> **Remount memory card.** Because a disk image is a duplicate of the original camera memory card, when you open the disk image, you'll see essentially the same thing (a volume) as when you originally mounted the camera memory card through a memory card reader or if you directly attached the camera to your computer.

Creating disk images is free, and you can use the tools that you already have on your Mac. Let's take a look at how easy it is to create a disk image.

1. Mount a camera memory card to your computer via a memory card reader or USB cable attached to your camera.

2. After the card has mounted, navigate to your Applications folder on your system drive and then to the Utilities folder (Shift+Command+U). In the Utilities folder, locate the Disk Utility application and double-click it to launch it. We find it easiest to make a shortcut in the dock so we can quickly create backups without having to hunt for the Disk Utility application.

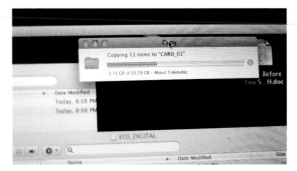

▲ Copying folders and files from a DSLR memory card to a portable drive is the easiest way to copy footage for backup purposes. However, there are a few problems with this method. It's possible that your files could be accidentally modified or deleted by the file system or another user. You must also be certain to copy all of the folders and files contained on the card.

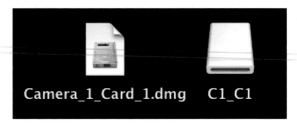

▲ Disk images are a great way to copy footage to portable drives while maintaining data integrity. They also offer the ability to remount camera memory cards.

▲ In the Disk Utility application you can easily make disk images of a selected volume.

▲ When you choose to create a disk image, you can name it, choose from different read and write options, as well as encrypt the disk image if necessary.

3. On the left side of the Disk Utility application, you'll see all of the volumes (drives) attached to your system. Notice that one of those items is the camera memory card you mounted in step 1. Select the volume, and then choose File > New > Disk Image from <<*Name*>> where <<*Name*>> represents the name of the camera memory card.

4. In the dialog that opens you can choose a location to save the disk image. If you're creating a disk image in the field, the best place to store that disk image is on a portable hard drive. You can also choose to name the disk image anything you want; however, we strongly suggest you use a standardized naming system like **Camera_1_Card_1.dmg** or something similar.

5. In the Image Format menu choose Read Only to prevent accidental modifications to the data.

6. In the Encryption menu choose None. Although you can encrypt a disk image in most cases, unless the content on a card is very sensitive, this just represents an extra step when you open the disk image.

7. Click Save. Depending on how large the memory card you're backing up is, the process of creating the disk image may take several minutes.

8. After the disk image as been created, be sure to mount the image and confirm it is good before reformatting and reusing your card. Once verified, you can eject the original camera memory card and reformat it in the camera for reuse.

HOW BIG WILL A DISK IMAGE BE?

In most cases, creating a disk image will create a file size that matches the original camera memory card size.

Selecting an Editing Drive

When it comes to editing, one of the major investments you'll need to make is a suitable editing drive. Forget single drive units. Although you can of course edit from a single drive, you won't have the capacity, speed, or redundancy you'll need for editing. Instead, consider the criteria discussed in the following sections when purchasing a media or edit drive.

RAID

You might have heard the term RAID (Redundant Array of Independent Disks) before. Basically, RAID is some fancy math that allows multiple drives to act as a single drive to the OS while offering various levels of redundancy. When it comes to redundancy and what are referred to as RAID levels, here is what you should know:

> **RAID 0** is a striped array, meaning that there is no redundancy, but speed and throughput is at its maximum.

> **RAID 1** is a mirrored array, meaning that if you have two 2 TB disks for a total of 4 TB, you'll only have 2 TB of actual storage. The other 2 TB is used as a mirror (or an exact copy of what is on the first disk on the RAID).

> **RAID 5** allows for parity data spread across disks, meaning that you can have one disk fail and you won't lose any data. You can rebuild the array. Think of this as magic: You don't have to know the math behind it, just that it works.

> **RAID 6** is similar to RAID 5 in the sense that parity data is spread across the array. But unlike RAID 5, you can actually lose two separate drives. RAID 6 is just like RAID 5, but twice as safe because you need three drive failures before you lose data.

Speed

Related to RAID levels is the speed of an array. Generally speaking, the more drives you have in an array, the faster the performance. Just keep in mind that the connectivity option that your array has also impacts the speed of the array. Speed performance will benefit you when you actually start to edit your project.

Connectivity

When it comes to your media (edit) drive, you'll want the latest and fastest connectivity that your computer supports. Connections like eSATA, USB 3.0, FireWire 800, and Thunderbolt are your best choices. Just keep in mind that depending on the type of connectivity you have, you may need to purchase additional hardware for your computer to interface with the latest drive connections. If you're using a tower or a 17-inch MacBook Pro, expansion slots make this easy. The addition of Thunderbolt on many new Macs also opens up a brave new world of speed.

▲ RAID arrays like this G-RAID from G-Technology provide fast and redundant storage.
©G-Technology by Hitachi Global Storage Technologies.

▲ Even portable drives like this G-RAID mini offer high-speed connections, such as FireWire 800 and eSATA.
©G-Technology by Hitachi Global Storage Technologies.

Transferring Media to an Edit Drive

After you've selected an appropriate media drive, the next step is to transfer your media from portable field storage to an edit drive. How you transfer data depends on how you've backed up that footage in the field. Your two choices include:

> **As folders and files.** If you've backed up your footage by copying folders and files from a camera memory card to a portable field drive, simply copy those folders and files to your media (edit) drive. Just be sure to copy every folder and file.

> **As disk images.** If you've created disk images of memory cards on your portable media drives, you'll first need to mount (by double-clicking) the .dmg files to mount the disk image(s). You can then tell Final Cut Pro X to copy the footage when you import.

After transferring media, you're ready to import and start editing media directly in Final Cut Pro X. In the next chapter you'll learn how to choose between native editing and transcoded workflows. Having a fast drive will be beneficial in both cases.

Creating Archives

After transferring media from field storage to your edit drives, we strongly recommend archiving that media in a format that is more long-term than portable field drives. The truth is that all hard drives fail. The spinning platters eventually give out and data loss occurs. Additionally, you'll probably want to reuse your portable field drives for other shoots.

The primary concern is that you don't want to be in the situation of not having a backup of your original footage if your edit drive should fail. To help solve this problem, you can create archives of your data from your portable drives. Generally, this is done after

transferring media to your media (edit drives), but you can also do so beforehand. Let's take a quick look at the formats that are often used for long-term archival of media and data.

Blu-ray Discs

Blu-ray Discs are a great choice for data archival in DSLR productions because the discs can hold 25 or 50 GB of data. Although the Blu-ray format is not natively supported on the Mac, that doesn't mean you can't create a Blu-ray data disc. Simply purchase an external Blu-ray burner (about $150) and Roxio Toast Titanium ($79) software, and you're ready to archive to Blu-ray. As of this writing, you can find 25 GB Blu-ray burnable discs (Bd-R) for as cheap as about $1.00 per disc.

DVD-ROM

You've probably been using and making DVD-ROMs for years. Since DVDs busted onto the scene in the mid-1990s, DVD-ROMs have become a simple and cheap way to archive data. The cool thing is, you most likely don't need any additional hardware or software on your Mac. Simply put a DVD-5 (about 4.3 GB) or DVD-9 (about 7.95 GB) disc into your machine, copy the files to the disc, and then burn the disc. The downside of using DVD-ROMs is their capacity. Although the capacity of DVD-5 or DVD-9 might seem like a lot, you can't back up the contents of a 16, 32, or 64 GB memory card on one DVD-ROM. However, with a bit of tactical planning about your backup strategy, you can use DVD-ROMs effectively.

▲ Blu-ray Discs are a great archiving option due to their storage capacity and relatively low cost.

Importing and Transcoding Your Media

The first step in editing is bringing your footage, stills, and audio into Final Cut Pro X. Although this may seem like a simple step (just drag and drop, right?), it actually involves many choices. You have several ways to access your files as well as several important decisions to make.

Do you want to work with the native camera files or optimized ProRes media? Should you analyze your clips to speed up the audio repair and color grading stages of your production? Would extra metadata and clip analysis speed up your editing as you search for the perfect shot?

Choices, choices, and more choices. Let's start making them and get to the fun part of editing.

Configuring Import Preferences

We strongly recommend that you take the time to set up your Import Preferences in Final Cut Pro X. These settings are used whenever you drag media from the Finder (as well as Aperture and iPhoto) into Final Cut Pro X. These preferences also serve as the default settings when you use the Import Files window (although in this case you can override them).

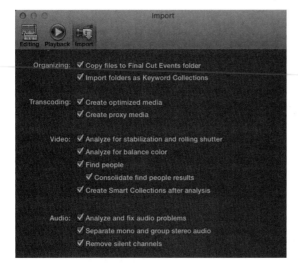

There are four categories of preferences that you need to make decisions about. Let's properly configure the Import Preferences.

1. If it's not running already, launch Final Cut Pro X.

2. Choose Final Cut Pro > Preferences.

3. Click the Import tab.

4. Make changes using the information in the following sections to guide you.

5. When you're finished, click OK to store your settings.

Organizing

To simplify your library and make it easier to manage, Final Cut Pro X offers two choices. Be sure to carefully consider your options here, or you can end up using a lot of disk space:

> **Copy files to Final Cut Events folder.** This option duplicates your media files and places them into the Final Cut Events folder. By default, this folder resides on your system drive. This choice is best if you're importing directly from removable media that will be disconnected or from memory cards that will be put back into the field.
>
> However, if you've already copied media to your edit drive as folders and files, this option creates an extra copy that may be unneeded (see "Transferring Media to an Edit Drive" in Chapter 2). Remember that Final Cut Pro X always transfers from cards and .dmg files (which it thinks are cards). We generally leave this check box deselected.

> **Import folders as Keyword Collections.** If you've taken the time to organize your footage into a folder structure with meaningful names, you should choose this option. Each folder or subfolder that a clip is nested inside will serve as a Keyword Collection. It is very useful to have this information (metadata) automatically attached to media in your Event Library. Final Cut Pro X will then sort your footage into Keyword Collections using this folder information. By default, we leave this check box selected.

 WHICH KEYWORDS ARE USED?
Keywords are only added for the current folder as well as any subfolders within it. Final Cut Pro X will not generate tags for folders above the one you are working with.

Transcoding

The decision to transcode is a multilayered one. Long-time Final Cut Pro editors are used to converting DSLR footage into Apple ProRes files to edit it. Doing so reduces the burden on the computer processors and graphics card, and instead transfers it to the high-bandwidth hard drive. A transcoded workflow means a less powerful computer can edit HD video, but the trade-off is a need for faster storage and more of it. If you are working with a powerful computer, you may be able to skip transcoding (a big time-saver as well as cost savings in drive space).

It's important to note that Final Cut Pro X is the first version of the application to support several key technologies that enable true native editing. The application is 64 bit and multithreaded, meaning that it can address significantly more RAM and processor cores than earlier versions. Final Cut Pro X also supports the use of the Graphics Processing Unit (GPU). This can dramatically improve playback performance.

▲ If your Mac offers an upgrade to the graphics card, strongly consider it. The GPU can dramatically improve the performance of Final Cut Pro X.

Here are the two choices related to transcoding:

> **Create optimized media.** The optimized media option transcodes the video to the Apple ProRes 422 codec, which can lead to better performance on less powerful systems.

> **Create proxy media.** Another choice is to make lower-quality transcoded media with the Apple ProRes 422 (Proxy) codec. This format is useful for offline editing tasks. This option is best for slower desktops and is especially well suited for laptops.

When you choose to transcode, Final Cut Pro X will always keep a copy of the original media for you to use at any time, such as for export. You can return to your source files at any time. You can also reconnect from an offline edit that used proxy media.

▲ You can track the progress of transcoded (optimized) footage by opening the Background Tasks window (Command+9).

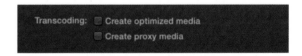

So what's the right choice? Well, we try to leave both options deselected and stay native. We usually have the benefit of a fast machine and prefer the use of less disk space, which makes it easier to move, back up, and transport our projects.

WHEN WILL OPTIMIZED MEDIA BE CREATED?

If the "Create optimized media" option is selected, transcoding does not occur with formats that are already optimized for editing, which include DV, DVCAM, DVCPRO HD, and other flavors of ProRes.

Analyzing Video

One of the major benefits of Final Cut Pro X is its ability to create and utilize a great deal of useful metadata. The application can automatically analyze still and video content. This analysis happens as a background process, which means that you can start using the footage before the analysis is complete.

You can use the data for a variety of tasks, including balancing color, removing camera shake, and repairing audio. The composition of a shot can also be analyzed to identify the number of people in a shot as well as its framing.

Here are the analyzation choices available:

> **Analyze for stabilization and rolling shutter.** Two problems that frequently plague DSLR video are shaky footage and rolling shutter. The camera shake is frequently caused by poor ergonomics when shooting with a DSLR camera. Rolling shutter is a side effect of the CMOS-style sensors and fast panning (it can lead to a bending of strong vertical lines in the image). If either of these problems is detected on import, you can correct the problem after you drag the clip into your Timeline. Because of the likelihood for both problems to exist, we recommend turning on this option.

> **Analyze for balance color.** This option looks for color casts and contrast issues in imported clips. After you drag a clip to the Timeline, you can enable the Balance Color option in the Inspector or press Option+Command+B. We'll

explore this option in-depth in Chapter 9, "Fixing and Enhancing Footage." We recommend leaving this option selected.

> **Find people.** You can use this option to determine the number of people in a shot as well as the composition of the shot (close-up shot, medium shot, etc.). A useful option here is to select "Consolidate find people results" to average out the counting (it basically analyzes two-minute chunks of video so you can avoid counting crew or unintended passersby). We find these two options to be relatively useful.

> **Create Smart Collections after analysis.** If you want to make your Find People analysis more useful, we recommend selecting this option. By creating a Smart Collection, you can quickly locate similar clips by using software-generated collections inside an event.

▲ Even using a stabilizing rig, small, unwanted movements may make it into your shot. Be sure to take advantage of the stabilization options in Final Cut Pro X.

GRAPHIC CONVERSION

The "Create optimized media" option also recompresses still images. Graphics without an alpha channel are converted to JPEG files. Those with an alpha channel or transparency are converted to PNG files. We feel that both of these formats have significant trade-offs compared to options like Photoshop (.psd) and Tagged Image File Format (.tif). Unfortunately, Final Cut Pro doesn't give you a choice, but you can go back to editing with original high-quality media at any time.

DON'T WANT TO SLOW DOWN IMPORT?

Don't worry; clip analysis happens as a background process, so you can start working with your footage right away. You can choose to analyze video during the import stage or analyze video clips later by Control-clicking in the Event Browser or in a project's Timeline. Although analyzing is truly a background task, it can slow down performance a bit. Also, some functions of the application may not be available until background tasks are completed or paused. So use your judgment, and just don't select all of the analysis options on import. Keep in mind that if you want to begin editing right away, you can perform all of these analyses at any time.

Analyzing Audio

Analyzing audio in your footage can help compensate for the challenges of acquiring good audio with DSLR cameras. Final Cut Pro X can fix common audio problems. You can analyze during import or afterward by Control-clicking a clip in the Event Browser or in the Timeline.

Final Cut Pro provides three audio analysis preferences:

> **Analyze and fix audio problems.** This catch-all category actually fixes several potential problems. Final Cut Pro looks for hum, unwanted background noise, and variations in loudness. The most problematic areas are marked in red, and moderate problems are marked in yellow. We discuss how to use this data in Chapter 10, "Working with Audio." We recommend leaving this option selected.

> **Separate mono and group stereo audio.** This option analyzes and groups audio channels. The available choices are Mono, Stereo, 5.1 surround, and 7.1 surround. This auto detection works well, but you can always force a change to the channel configuration by using the Channel Configuration section of the Audio inspector: Just choose the desired option from the Channels menu. We recommend leaving this option selected.

AUDIO UNDO

If you change your mind about how an audio clip is configured, simply click the Reset button in the Channel Configuration section of the Audio inspector.

Audio: ☑ Analyze and fix audio problems
☑ Separate mono and group stereo audio
☐ Remove silent channels

▲ The audio quality of DSLR footage is often challenging at best. The analysis tools in Final Cut Pro X are a big time-saver.

> **Remove silent channels.** If an imported clip doesn't have audio, you can tell Final Cut Pro X to remove any unused channels. This is useful if you record to only one channel on a stereo recording device or if your audio recorder has more than two recording channels. Final Cut Pro X will discard them so you don't have to. We typically recommend turning on this option only when you need it. We usually leave this option deselected.

Understanding Events

The key to organizing your imported media is to utilize events. An event can hold as few or as many video, audio, and image files as you like. One way of thinking of events is as a traditional folder or a bin. Unlike previous versions of Final Cut Pro, each event in the Event Library directly maps to a folder that Final Cut Pro X creates on your disk drive.

The event folder will contain either a copy of the imported media or an alias linking to the original file. This functionality is controlled by the Organizing preference "Copy files to Final Cut Events folder." The event folder will contain any rendered files or transcodes that you tell Final Cut Pro X to create. A database file is used to keep track of where everything is stored.

Best Practices for Events

You can work with events in many ways. But before we get into specific steps for creating events, let's review some best practices:

> Name your events by using a highly descriptive and unique name. Avoid simply using names like interview and b-roll. Remember that events are

not project specific and should be easy to identify by their name. Many choose to use a single event for each project or even a client; others use multiple events. Organization is key, and you'll quickly learn what works best for you.

> Refine the organization within an event by using keywords and smart collections.

> Group events by Disk or by Date. To do so, just click the Action menu at the bottom of the Event Library (the gear-shaped menu).

> Group or arrange clips within an event by using a variety of criteria. To do so, click the Action menu at the bottom of the Event Library.

▲ You can organize events effectively by clicking the Action menu. Grouping events by date makes it easy to search chronologically, whereas grouping by disk can make it easier to keep projects separated by using a disk for each major project or client.

▲ Our video project has three major components: a concert, an interview, and miscellaneous b-roll. An event can be used to organize each. Because we've dedicated our entire drive to this project, it's easy to organize events with simple names. If you're mixing clients on a single drive, be sure to use more descriptive names like Minimus The Poet – B-Roll, Minimus The Poet Concert, and so on.

Creating an Event

Getting organized is essential to a successful edit. To organize footage, you'll need to create events. You have options for creating new events: You can create an event during the import stage. You can also create multiple events in advance to get your library better set up.

Let's create a new event.

1. If the Event Library is not visible, click the Event Library button (it's in the bottom-left corner of the Event Browser).

2. Choose File > New Event (Option+N).

   A new event is added to the library with today's date.

3. Type a new name for the event and press Return.

RENAMING AN EVENT

While working with a project, you may decide that you want to rename an event. Simply click on an event's name in the Event Library and type a new name. Remember that renaming an event also changes the folder's name on your hard drive. If a background task is running on an event, its name cannot be changed until the task is completed.

Import Methods

Final Cut Pro X offers several methods for importing media. Many of these are specific to the device chosen or the format you shot on. With DSLR footage, you can import in a few ways: from the camera, memory card, or backed-up data. You can also import from your Aperture or iPhoto library.

To bring in media from your DSLR camera, Final Cut Pro X needs to see your memory card (real or a disk image). For best results, the entire folder structure that's been created by the camera should be intact. Final Cut Pro X can see the data in three ways:

› **Removable media.** The best way to transfer the data from your DSLR is to remove the memory card from the camera and connect it directly to your computer. Ideally, you'll use a fast card reader connection protocol, such as FireWire 800 or the built-in SD card slot on iMacs or MacBook Pros.

› **Direct connect.** If a card reader is not handy, you can connect your DSLR camera directly to your Mac. The most common connection type is USB 2.0. However, this method has two drawbacks: USB 2.0 tends to transfer slower than some of the other cable types, and this method is also hard on your camera because the ports can wear and the internal circuits on your camera can be damaged.

› **Aperture or iPhoto.** If you want to use one of Apple's photo management tools to also organize your video footage, you can do so. This is a common approach if you have mostly stills on a card.

› **Camera archive.** Certain cameras record media that needs to be treated as a camera archive. In the DSLR space, this is particular true for hybrid cameras like the Panasonic AG-AF100 as well as other models that shoot to the AVCHD format. An archive is a backup copy of the contents of a memory card.

CREATE A CAMERA ARCHIVE

You can create a camera archive within Final Cut Pro X. In the Camera Import window, select the device whose content you want to archive from the list of cameras on the left (most DSLR cameras will not appear). Then click the Create Archive button at the bottom-left corner of the window and choose a target drive. It is a good idea to keep your archives on a different drive than where you store your edit media. The reason is that you can restore data after a drive failure. If you are mixing your DSLR footage with tape-based footage, the camera archive feature can create a digital backup of the tape that can be archived with the rest of your DSLR footage.

WHAT ABOUT OTHER ASSETS?

You can also import other digital files by choosing File > Import (such as extracted music tracks and graphics). In addition, you can use the Photos and Music and Sound Browsers to access media from your photo and music libraries.

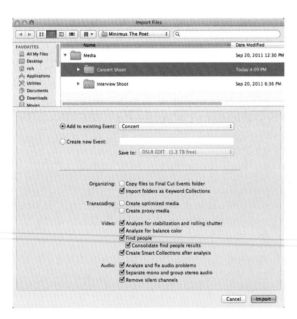

▲ The settings chosen by default in the Import Files window match the Import Preferences you learned about at the start of this chapter. You can modify these on an import-by-import basis directly in the window.

Importing Media from a Memory Card or Hard Drive

When it comes time to import DSLR footage, you need to create a scenario in which Final Cut Pro X can see the camera's memory card. You can connect the camera to your computer (likely using a USB cable), but be sure to power on the camera *after* you've connected it. Alternately, you can remove the memory card and place it into an attached card reader or use the internal SD card reader on many Macs. You can also use the media that you copied to your portable drive, which will give you the opportunity to copy the media to your edit drive (as discussed in Chapter 2).

Loading the media is easy.

1. In Final Cut Pro, choose File > Import > Files (Shift+Command+I).

2. Using the file navigation services, locate the DCIM folder on your camera's memory. Continue to drill down into nested folders until you find the actual movie files.

3. Command-click to select multiple files that you want to import.

4. Determine which event should hold the media:

   › If you'd like to use an existing event, choose "Add to existing Event" and select the event from the menu.

   › If you need to create a new event, choose "Create new Event." Type a name for the event into the text field, and choose a location to hold the event using the "Save to" menu. (If you make a mistake and create an extra Event Library, don't panic because you can easily combine libraries.

At the bottom of the Import window you'll find several options. These are selected or deselected based on the preferences discussed earlier in the chapter.

5. Adjust your import options to override the default preferences you've set.

6. Click Import.

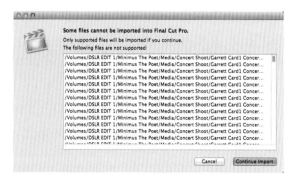

▲ You may have some files that cannot be imported into Final Cut Pro X. These are often extra files create by your camera that are unneeded for editing.

An error dialog may appear, especially if your media folders have other assets like thumbnail or extra data files. In this case, just ignore the error and click the Continue Import button.

The media starts to import as a background task. Any analysis or transcoding steps will occur after the initial import process is complete. If you want to check the status of any background tasks, press Command+9 to open the Background Tasks window.

UNWANTED KEYWORDS

If you selected the Import Folders as Keyword Collections option, you may get a few unwanted keywords. You can select these keywords in the Event Library list and press Command+Delete to remove them (don't worry; the media will not be deleted).

Understanding Disk Images

In Chapter 2 you learned how to make disk images. These are a very effective way to back up and store your data while ensuring that every bit of data on the camera card has successfully transferred. When it comes time to import this data into Final Cut Pro X, you have a few options:

> **Mount the disk image and transcode.** You can choose to mount the disk image by double-clicking it. It then appears as a media drive (just like a hard drive). When you choose File > Import > Files and navigate to the desired media, it's easy to bring in an event when you click Import. When you import, the footage will copy to the selected Final Cut Pro event folder with the settings specified in your Import Preferences.

> **Mount the disk image and copy.** If you choose to import the data from a disk image into an event, Final Cut Pro X will automatically copy the data. If you leave the optimize media options deselected, the data will come into your system in its native format.

> **Mount the card and copy.** An alternative to copying to your Final Cut Pro event is to use the Finder. You can mount the card and then copy the desired clips to a folder of your choice. When you choose File > Import > Files, simply make sure the option "Copy files to Final Cut Events folder" is deselected to avoid duplicating data.

> **Open the camera archive.** If you have a disk image of material that is AVCHD, you should first mount the card. Then choose File > Import from Camera. In the new dialog, click Open Archive, navigate to your disk image, and click Open. The footage will load into the window, and you can select clips for import.

Import from iPhoto and Aperture

You may already have footage that you've added to iPhoto or Aperture from a DSLR camera. Although we don't recommend this approach for large libraries, it is still useful to know that you can quickly grab photos or stills. You'll find specific instructions on importing media into iPhoto or Aperture in its Help menu. Let's discuss the two methods you can try to access the iPhoto and Aperture libraries in Final Cut Pro X.

DRAG TO IMPORT

You can drag your media from one application and drop it into another.

1. Launch iPhoto or Aperture.

2. Browse and locate the media you want to import.

3. Hold down the Command key and click to select multiple clips.

4. Drag the media onto the Final Cut Pro X icon in the dock and hover.

   A window appears showing Final Cut Pro X.

5. Drag the media over the application window and over the desired event.

6. When the event is selected, drop the media onto the event.

USE THE MEDIA BROWSER

An alternative is to use the Media Browser to access your iPhoto and Aperture libraries from within Final Cut Pro X. Any movies (as well as photos) that you've imported will be located in the Media Browser window.

1. Click the Photos button in the toolbar, or choose Window > Media Browser > Photos.

2. Navigate to the iPhoto or Aperture section of the Photos Browser.

A BETTER BROWSE

If you want to refine your photo or media search, click and hold on the iPhoto or Aperture menu. You can then choose from Events, Places, and Albums to refine your search for particular media.

3. Click to select the photos or video you want to use. You can hold down the Command key to select multiple items.

4. Drag the items from the Photos Browser to an event in the Event Library or a project in your Timeline.

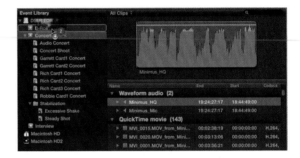

Import from a Camera Archive

When it comes to importing AVCHD media, you'll likely need to create a camera archive. Although similar to a disk image, the files in a camera archive are an exact copy of the media card. Remember that creating a camera archive from many DSLR cameras can't be done, but you may encounter camera archives with some of the other CMOS sensor-type cameras that are often used in DSLR-style workflows. In some cases, you can only see the mounted card by using the Import from Camera Archive feature.

After you've created a camera archive, there are two ways you can access the data:

> You can mount the archive on your drive and connect to the camera archive. This makes the media available in its native format to Final Cut Pro X. Even if the drive is mounted, you cannot use this media until you've connected to the camera archive and Final Cut Pro X detects it.

> You can import selected media from the camera archive. You can also import media from disk images that you've created with the old Final Cut Pro Log and Transfer window, Disk Utility, or other third-party tools. Working this way will create copies of the media on your local hard drive.

To use the media, Final Cut Pro X must first see the camera archive on your system.

1. Choose File > Import from Camera.

   The Camera Import window opens and shows you all connected cameras as well as camera archives in a list.

2. Decide which archive you want to use by selecting it:

   > Click to choose an archive in the list.

   > Click the Open Archive button, navigate to the folder you want to import, and click Open.

   You'll know that an archive is ready to use when the Eject icon appears to the right of the archive name. Media within an archive can be previewed using the playback controls. You can also skim the media with the pointer by dragging over its filmstrip.

3. Select the clips that you want to import, and choose an Import method:

   > Click Import All to bring in the entire archive.

   > A better choice is to select just the desired clips by Command-clicking each thumbnail and then clicking Import Selected.

   > To use just part of a clip, drag inside a clip to select the desired range.

LOG AND TRANSFER?

If you select a clip in a camera archive, you can better specify which parts you want to use. Simply select a clip in the Camera Archives window and press the spacebar to play the clip. You can then use the I key to set an In point and the O key to set an Out point.

4. Choose an event to hold your media.

   You can choose "Add to existing event" and specify the target using the menu. You can also choose "Create new event" and type a name.

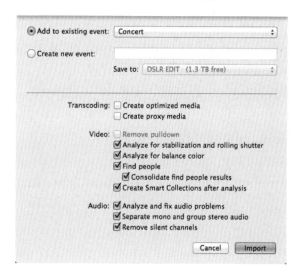

5. You can adjust your import options to override the default preferences you've set.

6. Click Import.

The media starts to import as a background task. Any analysis or transcoding steps will occur after the initial import process is complete. If you want to check the status of any background tasks, press Command+9 to open the Background Tasks window.

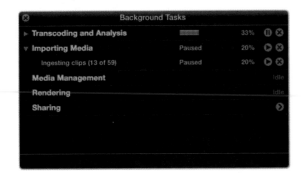

7. Close the Camera Import window to access the Event Browser.

You can now start working with the native media. Any transcoded media or analysis options will become available as the background tasks complete.

NO CAMERA ARCHIVE? NO WORRIES
The Open Archive command often works on folders of media as well. If you have media that the Files command (File > Import > Files) won't recognize, try the Open Archive command.

Understanding Your Transcoding Options

 When working with Final Cut Pro X, only two options for transcoding are readily available. By default, you can use Apple ProRes 422 by choosing the "Create optimized media" option in your preferences or the Import dialog. If you want a lower-resolution format for offline editing, you can use Apple ProRes 422 (Proxy) by choosing the "Create proxy media" option.

But what about the other three flavors of ProRes? You can import and use Apple ProRes 4444, Apple ProRes 422 (HQ), and Apple ProRes 422 (LT) if the media is created elsewhere. This means you can import media that was captured using direct-to-disk options like the AJA Ki Pro or captured using hardware cards and third-party software.

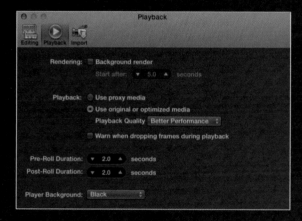

You can also bring media into Apple Compressor (a companion application sold separately through the Mac App Store). Here you'll find presets for Apple ProRes 4444 (good for embedded transparency) and Apple ProRes 422 (HQ) (which is good for 10-bit video files, not DSLR footage). If you want to use Apple ProRes 422 (LT), you'll need to create your own compression preset.

So which version of the media is used? That all depends on your preferences (your Playback preferences to be exact). Choose Final Cut Pro > Preferences and click the Playback button. You then have the option to either "Use proxy media" or "Use original or optimized media." Remember that Final Cut Pro X will switch from the camera native files to the optimized ProRes media when the background conversion is complete or the optimized media is detected.

Here's how to choose which video quality is used by Final Cut Pro X:

> High Quality uses the native media formats on your drive.

> Better Performance uses optimized media if available. Final Cut Pro X typically optimizes media for Long GOP-type media formats like H.264, HDV, and AVCHD formats.

> You can also choose "Use proxy media" to improve performance. If you haven't created proxy media on import (or by using the File > Transcode Media option) your clips will appear offline. Simply switch the Playback preference back to "Use original or optimized media."

the "good parts"—the best sound bites, the most expressive b-roll, and the shots that just work. Of course, you then have to figure out how to put all of those pieces together.

In a sense, the act of editing video is much like having ten different jigsaw pieces mixed together. You have to find the right pieces and figure out how they go together while ignoring the pieces you don't need.

Let's just say that getting organized will be a critical step in your journey to a compelling story. Fortunately, Final Cut Pro X has several tools that let you sort, sift, filter, and find the perfect shot. You can use embedded metadata as well as attach powerful keywords to improve your ability to locate the perfect shot.

In this chapter we'll explore the many ways to organize your media. Although you may want to skip ahead, we encourage you to tough it out. Learning how to organize an edit will make the whole process run faster and ensures that you'll have the best shots at your fingertips.

Examining Events

After you've imported media into events, you'll want to explore the content at your fingertips. Any video, audio, or still images that you've imported will appear as clips in one or more events.

Final Cut Pro X is very literal when it comes to your media inside an event. Each event in the Event Library has a matching folder on your hard drive. Inside each folder is the actual imported media (or an alias that points to the original file).

Sorting Events

As you import your media, you'll likely end up with multiple events. As you learned in Chapter 3, "Importing and Transcoding Your Media," it is common practice to organize events by factors like shoot date, client, or topic.

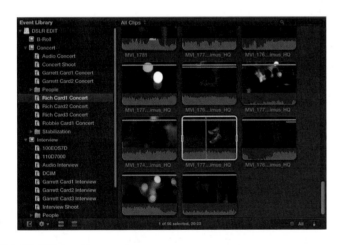

▲ Clicking the Action menu (which is shaped like a gear) gives you access to several different sorting methods for events.

You need to find a level of comfort with events, deciding how big you want each event to be and how broad a range each event should cover. For example, for the project we're using in this book, we're using a single, dedicated drive for the project, and footage will be grouped into three events: Concert, Interview, and B-roll.

As you work with events, it's important to use the many organizational tools offered by Final Cut Pro X. You can access all of the sort methods by clicking the Action menu (just look for the gear icon below the Event Library):

› **Sort events by date.** If you're working on a project that has many shooting days, sorting by date can be useful. Just click the Action menu and choose Group Events by Date. You can sort by Year, Year and Month, or choose not to group.

HIDING EVENTS

There are also many ways that you can choose to hide old or nongermane events in the Event Library. For example, you can unmount the drive that holds the media or move the event out of the Movies folder on your drive. We'll fully explore these workflows in Chapter 11, "Outputting and Managing Your Project."

WHY ARE MY EVENTS IN 1969?

It's very easy to have an incorrect creation date. Perhaps you didn't set the time on your camera or audio recorder when you changed batteries. Perhaps the clock was wrong on your computer. If you have one clip in your event with a different creation date, the event will automatically sort itself based on the oldest asset. For this reason we recommend not sorting events by date because it isn't always accurate. We choose either the Don't Group Events by Date option or Show Event Date Ranges for greater accuracy.

CHANGE THE CREATION DATE

A useful application for adjusting creation dates is A Better Finder Attributes from www.publicspace.net. Because this kind of tool alters the media files, it is best to use it before importing into Final Cut Pro.

◀ There are several ways to sort events. From left to right, Group Events by Disk, Group Events by Year, and Group Events by Month and Year.

> **Sort events by storage location.** Many choose to isolate clients or projects by hard drive. If you're using multiple disks or partitions, sorting by location is a good idea. Just click the Action menu and choose Group Events by Disk. This option can be combined with any of the date sorting options.

> **Show event date ranges.** If you want to see the full range of dates an event contains, you can choose Show Date Ranges in Event Library from the Action menu. This can help you easily find footage within events by date.

> **Sort events by most recent.** If you want to see the newest footage first, choose Arrange Events by Most Recent from the Action menu.

Viewing Events as a Filmstrip

If you are visually oriented, you'll find the Filmstrip view very useful. By displaying the event as a filmstrip, you can see several frames that represent the contents of your footage. For many, this is the easiest way to visually browse media (especially because clips from DSLR cameras lack descriptive names).

1. If a List view is shown, click the "Show clips in filmstrip view" button near the bottom of the Event Browser.

2. Drag the duration slider to adjust the number of frames shown for each clip's thumbnail in the Event Browser. You can also press Shift+Z to zoom to fit each clip to a single thumbnail. Usually, setting the duration to 5–10 seconds works well. But your mileage may vary depending on the type of footage and length of shots you are working with.

3. If you want to adjust what's shown in each thumbnail, click the Clip Appearance button at the bottom-right corner of the Event Browser. You can adjust the height of the clip as well as disable the audio waveform.

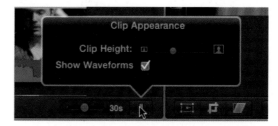

Viewing Events as a List

If you prefer to organize your footage by file details like creation date, duration, or keyword, you'll find the List view useful. Although the List view is mostly filled with sortable columns, there is a large filmstrip preview at the top of the window. This filmstrip allows full access to all of the media as well as the ability to use markers and keyword ranges.

1. If a Filmstrip view is shown, click the "Show clips in list view" button near the bottom of the Event Browser.

2. To customize which columns are viewable, Control-click on any column heading and choose a category option from the menu.

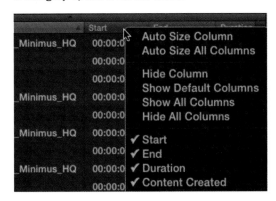

3. To rearrange columns, click a column heading and hold. You can then drag a column left or right if you prefer a different order.

4. To sort a column, click its heading.

You can click a second time to toggle between ascending and descending sort order.

5. To view a clip's rating or keywords, just click the disclosure triangle to the left of the clip's name.

Sorting Clips within Events

As you continue to review your events, it's easy to become overwhelmed by all your footage (especially with a big project). Fortunately, Final Cut Pro X offers several additional ways to refine how your events display clips. Much like sorting events, you can sort clips within an event. It all begins by clicking the Action menu:

› **Group Clips By Category.** You can choose Group Clips By and select from several methods, including Reel, Date, Scene, Duration, File Type, and more. You can set the order to Ascending or Descending from the same submenu to create a hierarchy. We find that grouping by File Type is extremely useful because it groups audio, video, and graphics separately.

› **Arrange Clips By Category.** You can also arrange clips by Name, Take, Duration, and Content Created. We find the last method (Content Created) useful because it sorts clips in order of creation. If you've manually renamed media, the Name option is also useful. Arrangements can also be sorted in Ascending or Descending order.

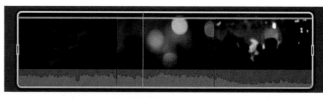

◀ The J-K-L keys will quickly become an integral part of your keyboard controls.

▲ Grouping by category is a useful way to organize your media.

THE BEST OF BOTH

You can use both a Group and an Arrange method to sort clips independent of each other. Using these arrangement features makes it much easier to find clips.

Examining Clips

Now that you have control over sorting your clips, it's time to actually watch your media. The process of reviewing or skimming your footage will make it easier to tag footage with keywords and roles, as well as help you find the best shots.

Taking the time to review your footage and annotate it greatly improves your end results. When an event is selected in the Event Library, you can view its clips in the Event Browser. This is the first step toward viewing and organizing your footage.

Viewing Individual Clips

When you've located a clip in an event, you have several ways to view its contents. It's important that you learn how to use the dynamic preview capabilities of Final Cut Pro X to speed up your edit workflow.

There are two primary tools that you'll use for playback and previewing: the playhead and the skimmer.

PLAYHEAD

The playhead indicates your current position within a project. The playhead appears as a thin, gray vertical line. Generally, the playhead is static, but you can reposition it by clicking in a clip or your Timeline. The playhead does move when you click Play to indicate progress as a clip or Timeline plays back.

Here are a few tips to control playback:

> Press the spacebar to start or stop playback.

> To play a clip from its beginning, press Shift+Control+I.

> To play just a part of a clip, click and drag the yellow handles to define a frame range. Press the Forward Slash (/) key to play just the selected part of the clip.

> If you do not select a range, you can still press Shift+Forward Slash (/) to play two seconds before and after where the playhead is parked.

> You can use the J-K-L keys to control playback:

>> Press L to play forward.

>> Press J to play backward.

>> Press K to pause the video clip.

>> To double the playback speed, tap L or J twice. Tap again for further incremental speed changes.

> To move the playhead one frame at a time, hold down the K key and tap J or L.

> To move the playhead in slow motion, hold down the K key while pressing down J or L.

WANT TO THINK ABOUT IT?
If you want to keep playing a clip over and over again to closely study it, that's easy. Just press Command+L to toggle looping on or off.

SKIMMER

Another method for previewing clips is the skimmer. Using the skimmer lets you move the mouse to freely preview a clip without affecting the playhead position. The benefit of the skimmer is that it lets you quickly review several frames in a clip by simply moving the mouse (all without losing your current position).

The skimmer appears as a thin, pink vertical line as you move the pointer across the clip. The skimmer temporarily turns orange if snapping is enabled and the skimmer snaps to a position. Snapping makes it easier to drag between markers and In points, for example.

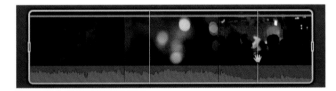

THE TROUBLE WITH SKIMMING
When it comes to skimming, you'll either love it or hate it, or sometimes both. The good news is that you can enable or disable skimming easily. You can turn off all skimming by pressing S or audio skimming only by pressing Shift+S.

SWITCH FROM SKIM
If you want to play a clip while skimming, just press the spacebar. The playhead will jump to the skimmer position and start to play.

Renaming Clips

By default, DSLR media has pretty useless filenames (they're not unique, and it's very easy to have duplicate filenames). Even if all your files have different names, how useful is a name like MVI_04567.mov? Fortunately, you can easily rename clips within your event. You can rename clips in the Event Browser or in the Info inspector anytime you want. Note that when you rename a clip in Final Cut Pro X, it *does not* rename the source media file on your disk. Here are a few ways you can rename clips:

> **Rename a clip in the Event Browser in Filmstrip view.** If you're in Filmstrip view, simply select a clip's name and type a new name.

> **Rename a clip in the Event Browser in List view.** If you're in List view, simply select a clip's name, press Return, and then type a new name.

> **Rename a clip in the Info inspector.** Select a clip in the Info inspector by clicking the Inspector button in the toolbar. Click the Info button at the top of the pane that appears. You can then click in the Name field and type a new name.

Organizing Clips with Roles

When you import clips into Final Cut Pro X, the application automatically assigns metadata text labels. These labels are based on one of five default roles: Video, Titles, Dialogue, Music, or Effects. You can also create custom roles and further refine with subroles that you can manually assign to clips. For example, you can assign the role of Interview to all of your sound bites to easily separate them from the rest of your footage.

WHAT A NAME DOES
When you rename a clip, it only affects the one instance of the clip. For example, if you copy a clip from one event to another and then rename one of the clips, only the modified clip will change. Every instance of a clip can have its own name.

Apple has positioned roles as the primary way to identify related elements when working in the Timeline and when exchanging data with an XML file. Roles should continue to play a more important part as Final Cut Pro X continues to evolve and share media with other applications.

SETTING UP ROLES

A good place to start to set up roles is to open the Roles Editor. Choose Modify > Edit Roles to see the current roles and subroles you've set up. Roles are globally defined for the application, so you cannot have different roles for different projects.

To create a new role, follow these steps.

1. To add a new role, click the Assign New Role button at the bottom-left corner of the Role Editor window.

2. Choose to add a New Video Role or New Audio Role.

3. Click on the new role and enter a new name.

You can also add subroles to further refine a role category. For example, you can split the Video role into smaller categories like b-roll, behind the scenes, reenactment, and so on to make it easier to categorize your footage. Creating subroles is easy.

1. Click a role to select it.

2. Click the Subrole button at the bottom center of the panel.

3. Click on the new subrole and enter a new name.

THE RULES

Keep in mind that there are a few rules when it comes to using roles:

> Every clip must have at least one assigned role.

> If a clip has audio and video, it will always have one audio and one video role.

> You cannot assign a video role to audio-only clips or an audio role to video-only clips.

> Roles cannot be assigned to a clip range or a portion of a clip.

> You can assign different roles to each instance of a clip. For example, a clip in the Timeline can have a different role assigned in an event.

> To delete a subrole or a custom role, just click to select it and press the Delete key. You cannot delete the original five roles, however. You'll also need to make sure that no clips are assigned to a subrole in your events. Once cleared, the role or subrole will no longer appear as an option when you relaunch the application.

ASSIGNING ROLES

You can assign roles to clips at any point in your editing. In fact, you can assign a role in the Event Browser, the Info inspector, the Modify menu, or the Timeline Index. Here's how:

> **View and reassign roles in the Event Browser.** With one or more clips selected in the Event Bowser, you can use the Roles column. Make sure you are in List view and that you can see the Roles column (if it's not visible, Control-click a column head and choose Roles). You can then click the assigned role for a clip to see a shortcut menu listing the available roles. Simply choose additional roles that you want to assign.

> **View and reassign roles in the Info inspector.** With one or more clips selected in the Event Bowser or Timeline, you can use the Info inspector. If it's not visible, click the Inspector button in the toolbar and click the Info button at the top of the pane that appears. You can click in the Roles field to choose from available roles.

> If the Roles metadata is not visible, click the View button at the bottom of the pane and choose Edit Metadata View. You can then use the search field and enter roles. Select the Roles field to add it to your view.

> **View and reassign roles in the Modify menu.** An easy way to assign roles is to use the Modify menu. With a clip selected, simply choose Modify > Assign Roles, and choose a role from the submenu. Once selected, a check mark appears next to the roles in use.

> **Use keyboard shortcuts.** If you want to assign roles using the keyboard, that's possible too:
> > Video (Control+Option+V)
> > Titles (Control+Option+T)
> > Dialogue (Control+Option+D)
> > Music (Control+Option+M)
> > Effects (Control+Option+E)

> **View and reassign roles in the Timeline Index.** After you've added clips to a Timeline, you can assign roles. This function is often used to help assign track-based output for files (such as when going to tape). You can also use roles to help you isolate clip types in your Timeline (even making entire roles invisible by deselecting them).

> Open the Timeline Index by pressing Command+Shift+2. View your clips in use by clicking the Clips pane at the top of the Timeline index. Use the Roles column to add roles to your clips (if it's not visible, just Control-click on the heading and choose Roles from the menu). You can then click on a role and add or edit assigned roles.

Managing Your Event Library

Now that you understand the value of events as an organizational tool, it's important to know how to manage your Event Library. There are several ways to merge, split, and rename events.

Merging Events

If you end up with too many events, you can quickly merge two or more events into a single event. This makes sense if you have two events with media that is closely related (such as by client or topic).

There are two ways to merge events:

> You can select multiple events that you want to combine, and choose File > Merge Events. In the Merge Events window, give the event a new name, choose a disk where you want to store the event's source media files from the Location menu, and click OK.

> You can create and name a new event, and then drag one or more existing events into the new (empty) event.

Splitting Events

If you find that an event is getting too big to manage, you can split it into two events. There are two strategies you can employ to make this task simple:

> You can create a new event and drag the media from its current event into a new event. The original media files (or aliases) on your disk will be moved into the new Events folder.

> You can choose to create a duplicate event and modify it by highlighting the desired event and choosing File > Duplicate Event. You can then go through the event and delete any unwanted clips. Simply select an unwanted clip (or clips) and press Command+Delete to remove it from the event and your disk. Be careful not to just press Delete (which seems natural): Instead of removing a clip, you will just mark the clip as "Rejected."

Copying Media Between Events

When you want to have a clip appear in two events, you can copy it. This will place a version of the clip in both events, which means that files are duplicated on disk. To copy the clip:

> If the event is on the same disk, hold down the Option key when dragging.

> If the events are on different disks, simply drag.

You'll know that a copy is occurring if a green circle with a plus symbol appears next to the clip's name when dragging.

Moving Media Between Events

When you want to take a clip from one event and put it in another, you can choose to move it. This means that the file will actually be removed from one folder on your disk and relocated to another. To move a clip:

> If the event is on the same disk, simply drag from one event to another.

> If the events are on different disks, hold down the Command key when you drag.

You'll know that a move is occurring if no symbol appears next to the clip's name when dragging. It's important to note that this actually moves the clip from one drive to another at the Finder level. This could be dangerous if you are sharing media.

WHAT'S THE WAIT?
Keep in mind that when you copy or move media, files are actually transferring in the background. If you are managing a lot of media, it can take a few minutes to complete the task of copying or moving the source files from disk to disk.

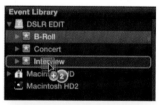

◀ The plus symbol indicates a copy command is in progress.

▲ The lack of a plus symbol (number of files is in a red circle) indicates that a Move command has been invoked.

Rating Clips

Now that you've figured out how to browse your events and organize your content, it's time to start making decisions. You need to rate your clips so you know which ones you want to use and which ones you should ignore. Final Cut Pro X has a three-choice system of ratings.

> All clips come in at a neutral state.

> You can then mark your favorite clips (or star them) to be sure to use them.

> You can also reject a clip and hide it to avoid using footage that is subpar.

Marking Favorite Clips

As you review your footage, you'll want to take the time to mark the best shots you want to use, making it easier to find those shots while you're in the middle of an editing session (especially if the client is in the room). Marking favorites gives you a quick way to isolate your best footage.

1. In the Event Browser, select a clip, or multiple clips, you want to rate.

   You can also use the Select tool to choose a range (part) of a clip. This is similar to the process of creating a subclip.

2. Press F or click the Favorite button in the toolbar.

   A green line appears at the top of the frames you've marked as Favorite in the Event Browser.

 YOU'RE NOT MY FRIEND ANYMORE
If you change your mind about a Favorite ranking, that's easy to amend. Just press the U key (for un-favorite) or click the Remove Ratings from the Selection button in the toolbar. To quickly reselect just the range, click the green bar or red bar.

▶ By making a selection and pressing the F key, you can mark that selection as a favorite for quick reference later.

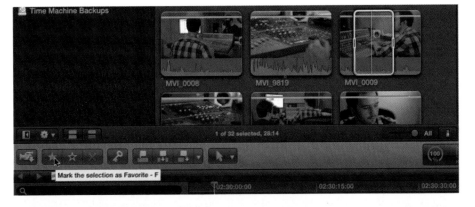

▶ The green bars indicate regions that have been marked as favorites. The red bar shows a clip that has been rejected.

Rejecting Clips

Just as you mark your best clips, you should also take the time to reject those shots you want to avoid. The Rejected rating should be used for shots that contain soft focus, bad performance, or garbled audio.

▲ Remember that Delete rejects a clip, whereas Command+Delete throws it in the trash (these are the same shortcuts used in the Finder).

1. In the Event Browser, select a clip, or multiple clips, you want to rate.

   You can also use the Select tool to choose a range (part) of a clip.

2. Press Delete or click the Rejected button in the toolbar.

   A red line appears at the top of the frames you've marked as Rejected in the Event Browser.

Removing Ratings

If you want to remove the rating from a clip, it's pretty simple. At the top-left corner of the Event Browser, click the Filter menu and choose the All Clips option to ensure that you are seeing all of your footage. You can then press U or click the Clear Rating button in the toolbar. This removes the green or red line at the top of the clips in the Event Browser.

Filtering Clips

Ratings are very useful for several tasks. You can use the Filter menu in the Event Library or corresponding keyboard shortcuts to adjust your view. This makes it easier to edit by removing substandard shots. It's also a great way to clean up an event.

▲ The view on the left is the standard icon view of the event in All Clips mode (Control+C). On the right, only Favorites are shown (Control+F).

Here are a few ways to get organized using the Filter menu:

> You can choose to display just the clips that are marked as Favorites by pressing Control+F.

> If you want to hide the Rejected clips, press Control+H.

> If you need to free up disk space, press Control+Delete to see only your Rejected clips. You can then select this media and press Command+Delete to remove it from the event and your hard drive. For more information, see "Deleting Footage" at the end of this chapter. Just be careful; if a media file contains both Favorite and Rejected ranges, all the media is discarded with this method.

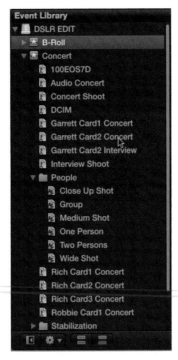

▲ The purple keywords are generated by Final Cut Pro X when you analyze imported media. The blue keywords were added on import or using the Keyword Editor.

Adding Keywords to Clips

Another tool at your disposal for organizing media is the use of keywords. You can use two types of keywords when working in Final Cut Pro X:

> **Analysis keywords.** Final Cut Pro X can automatically generate keywords when you analyze clips for common problems. This can be done on import or after the fact when you select clips in an event and choose Modify > Analyze and Fix.

> **Manually added keywords.** You can also review clips and choose to add keywords of your own design. This is a great way to get organized based on repeating themes or logical groupings.

NEED MORE DETAILS?

Keywords are very useful, but sometimes you'll want more details. When working in List view for an event, you'll find a Notes column. Here you can add detailed information about a clip. Notes can also be assigned to any Keyword or Favorite ranges by clicking the disclosure triangle and then clicking in the Notes column for each item.

Assigning Keywords

Adding keywords is a very straightforward process (and one that will seem familiar if you use iPhoto or Aperture). Make sure you either watch your footage playback in real time or use the skimmer to quickly browse.

1. In the Event Browser, make a selection. You can choose a range, an entire clip, or multiple clips that you want to add keywords to.

2. Click the Keywords button in the toolbar to open the Keyword Editor.

3. Enter a word or phrase that you want to use as a keyword for the selected clip(s) and press Return.

4. Continue adding keywords or keyword phrases as needed.

A blue line appears at the top of the selection in the Event Browser, which indicates that keywords are in use for the clip or range.

5. When you're finished adding keywords, simply close the Keyword Editor.

As you continue to add keywords to your clips, you'll see more Keyword Collections appear in the Event Library. A Keyword Collection is essentially a group of pointers (aliases) to clips that you have tagged with a specific keyword.

Using Keyword Shortcuts

Another quick way to add keywords or keyword phrases is to use keyboard shortcuts. You can have up to nine shortcuts loaded globally (not per event). However, removing a shortcut does not affect clips you've already tagged. You can freely adjust your shortcut keys without affecting your previously processed footage.

MULTIPLE KEYWORDS
You can add multiple keywords to a shortcut register. Just press Tab and enter the new keyword. The shortcut will then apply multiple keywords with a single click.

Here's how to use keyword shortcuts.

1. If it's not already open, click the Keywords button in the toolbar to open the Keyword Editor.

2. If the shortcuts aren't visible, click the disclosure triangle to the left of Keyword Shortcuts in the Keyword Editor.

3. Click in a field next to a shortcut (1–9) and enter a phrase or keyword in a shortcut field. Press Return to capture the change.

4. To use a keyword shortcut, select a range or one or more clips that you want to modify.

5. Press Control and the corresponding number key (1 through 9) to assign a keyword or keyword phrase.

Removing Keywords

If you need to remove a keyword, you can do so in two ways. You can remove individual keywords or all keywords:

> **Remove individual keywords.** If you need to delete a keyword from a clip, just select it and open the Keyword Editor. You can then select and delete any keywords in the top field to adjust the clip or selection.

▲ Keywords were automatically added because the Import Folders as Keyword Collections option was selected. In this case a few clips were tagged incorrectly because the Director of Photography had footage from two days of shooting on one card.

> **Remove all keywords from a clip.** In the Event Browser, select one or more clips. Then choose Mark > Remove All Keywords (Control+0).

Filtering Clips

Now that you've taken the time to organize your footage into events, apply keywords and ratings, and analyze your footage, you have a lot of information to work with. Learning how to use the Filter commands will give you greater control while editing.

Search for Clips By Clip Names and Notes

Located at the top of the Events Library is the search field. This is a useful way to search for clips by name or by any notes you've added. Simply select one or

more events you want to search in the Event Library (Command-click for multiple events). Then in the search field enter a text string you want to search for. To remove a search, just click the small x at the right of the field.

Search for Clips By a Combination of Criteria

Although the search field is convenient, using a combination of criteria lets you quickly find the clips you're looking for. You can use multiple criteria to search with the Filter window. Categories include clip name, rating, media type, excessive shake, keywords, the presence of people, format information, date, and role.

1. In the Event Library, select the event or folder you want to search.

2. Click the Filter button at the top-right corner of the Event Browser.

► You can select unwanted keywords in the Keyword Editor and press Delete to remove them.

► Use the Search field (in the upper-right corner of the browser) to search the Name and Notes columns.

3. In the Filter window, select search criteria, or rules. You can add additional rules using the Add Rule menu:

> **Text.** Find clips by their name or search any notes applied to them in List view.

> **Ratings.** Find clips based on the rating assigned.

> **Media Type.** Search for clips whose source media files are of a specific type (video, audio, or stills).

> **Stabilization.** Hide or show video clips that Final Cut Pro has identified as having excessive shake.

> **Keywords.** Search for one or more keywords.

> **People.** Find clips that Final Cut Pro X has identified as having people in them if you analyzed your clips.

> **Format Info.** Search by frame rate, reel, take, scene number, and other criteria.

> **Date.** Search by creation or import date, as well as apply logical rules to help specify an exact match or a range of dates.

> **Roles.** Find clips by their assigned roles. Earlier in the section "Organizing Clips with Roles," you learned to assign custom roles and subroles, as well as how certain roles are automatically added.

4. You can refine a search by applying additional rules. You can specify that a search must match at least one criterion or that all criteria must be met. Just use the menu in the upper-left corner and choose All or Any.

5. When you're done with a search, click the Reset button to the right of the search status icons in the upper-right corner of the Event Browser.

▲ By refining the Filter controls, the clips were narrowed down to only those that contained the keyword mixer, were marked as favorites, and did not have excessive shake.

Using Smart Collections

The powerful search criteria in Final Cut Pro X really let you drill down through many clips to find the results you need. To make it easier to search, Final Cut Pro X lets you save your search results as a new Smart Collection. Clips that appear in Smart Collections are not duplicate media. Rather, Smart Collections filters clips in an event, which helps you focus on the clips needed for a specific task.

CREATE A SMART COLLECTION BASED ON SEARCH CRITERIA

To create a Smart Collection, select an event in the Event Library to begin.

1. Use the Filter window to perform a criteria-based search.

2. Click the New Smart Collection button in the Filter window to add an untitled Smart Collection in the Event Library.

3. Type to enter a new name for the Smart Collection, and press Return.

Whenever you add clips to an event that match the Smart Collection's search criteria, they will be automatically added to the Smart Collection.

CHANGE THE CONTENTS OF A SMART COLLECTION

After you've created a Smart Collection, you can still modify it.

1. Double-click a Smart Collection whose contents you want to change.

2. In the Filter window, modify the search criteria.

3. Close the Filter window to update the Smart Collection.

DELETE A SMART COLLECTION

If you decide that you no longer want a Smart Collection, select it and choose File > Delete Smart Collection (or press Command+Delete). This removes the Smart Collection from the Event Library but does not delete the associated clips.

▲ By storing a set of filter results as a Smart Collection, you make it easy to find your footage while in the midst of future editing sessions.

Deleting Footage

As you continue to edit your footage, you may decide to delete footage from an event. Unlike previous versions of Final Cut Pro (and most other nonlinear editing tools), deleting a clip from an event actual *does* move the source media to your computer's trash.

Deleting Media

If you want to remove individual clips, just select them in an event. Then choose File > Move to Trash (or press Command+Delete). If you're sure you want to permanently get rid of them, switch to the Finder and choose Finder > Empty Trash.

It's important to note that only media inside events will be trashed. If you did not copy the data into the event on import, the original media remains on your disk. For this reason, we do not select the Copy files to Final Cut Event folder option on import. In this workflow you'll delete the aliases that point to the media, but your original camera files will remain on disk. This workflow works well because the media might be in use in another project or another editor may need it (also, there's no danger of trashing your original media files).

If you're not sure you want to commit to deleting media, just reject it, and then choose Hide Rejected. You can easily recover rejected clips by removing the rating from the clip.

Deleting Events

Another option when cleaning up is to delete an entire event. This technique should not be used often because it is a quick way to clear off several clips that you no longer need. Typically, you'll want to back up or archive your media first, however. Be sure to read Chapter 11 to learn about managing projects and media before you start throwing away events or clips.

1. Select an event or multiple events in the Event Browser for deletion.

2. Choose File > Move Event to Trash (Command+Delete).

DANGER! DANGER!

If you move items to the trash and then empty the trash, those clips (and all their metadata) are gone for good. After you empty the trash, the deleted clips or event and all their source media files that previously resided in the Final Cut event cannot be recovered.

CHAPTER **5**

Setting Up
a Project

Did you jump to this chapter first?

We can't blame you, but we can warn you. Final Cut Pro X approaches the editing workflow very differently than other tools (including Final Cut Pro 7). You need to carefully read Chapters 3 and 4 before you will be ready to edit. All the time you spent organizing events will really pay off when it comes time to edit.

We think this change in mind-set for Final Cut Pro came from how Apple designed iPhoto and Aperture. In these workflows you bring in photo and video assets and then organize and tag them. When you're done, you can quickly gather the pieces into assembled content like slide shows and albums for sharing online.

So even though you haven't actually edited yet, remember this: A lot of work went into your media and events just to get you to this point—creating a project. If this is a bit confusing, we agree. So we'll break it down for you.

Final Cut Pro X Project Structure

Before we delve into the project structure for Final Cut Pro X, let's take a look back by first reviewing how other video editing tools store their data.

In previous versions of Final Cut Pro, you would first create a new project. You'd then start importing or transferring footage into your project. You'd use a folder or bin-based organization structure and add some notes along the way. This would capture all of the information about your media into a project. In fact, a Final Cut Pro 7 project included clips (with metadata and links to the source media) as well as sequences (which contained your editing decisions).

The good news is that you'll accomplish the same results in Final Cut Pro X. However, the way you'll go about doing so is a bit different. For all the footage you brought in so far in previous chapters, you've completed similar organizational tasks. Instead of organizing with bins, you've used events and keywords to tag your media. Unlike Final Cut Pro 7, this database you created isn't tied to any one project; it is available for all your projects (or just the project you are working on). We'll talk more about this in Chapter 11, "Outputting and Managing Your Project."

Once your media is organized, it's time to edit a project to arrange and sequence your clips (and tell a story). In most other editing programs you'd create a sequence. In Final Cut Pro X it's called a project. You can have as many projects as you need, but each project has a single sequence. Multiple projects can refer to the same media and metadata. **Table 5.1** compares the differences between Final Cut Pro 7 and Final Cut Pro X.

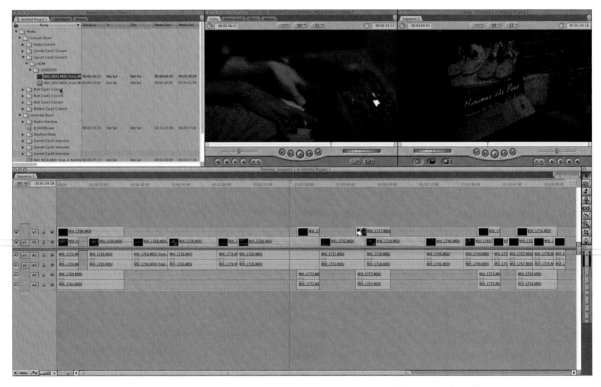

▲ A Final Cut Pro 7 project contains media (inside bins) and a sequence stored in one project file.

Table 5.1 Structural Differences Between Final Cut Pro 7 and Final Cut Pro X

FINAL CUT PRO 7	FINAL CUT PRO X
Bins	Events, Keyword Collections, and Smart Collections
Audio and Video Capture Scratch folder	Final Cut Events folder
Sequence	Project
Audio and Video Render Files folder	Final Cut Projects folder
Timeline	Timeline

Starting a Project

Before you create your project, we recommend that you revisit a few technical decisions. In Chapter 1, "Shooting with Editing in Mind," you learned about the many variations in frame size and frame rate. Now it's time to implement that knowledge. Be sure you can answer these three questions before moving forward:

> **What is my delivery frame size?** Are you delivering in HD? Is that 1920 x 1080 or 1280 x 720? Is the delivery for broadcast or output to tape? With many broadcast formats, you might be getting into non-square pixel dimensions (like 1440 x 1080). Always double-check with your client or technical contact. If you're just working on a personal project, you'll simply match the settings of your dominant frame size. It's important to note that if you are delivering a master file for HD, 1920 x 1080 will give your client the most options (it's easier to scale down than up while maintaining quality).

> **What is your delivery frame rate?** The choice of frame rate is another example of following standards. In Chapter 1 we reviewed your frame rate choices when shooting video. The goal is to maintain a consistent rate throughout the project.

> **What is your segmentation?** Chances are if you shot on a DSLR that you will edit and deliver a progressive file. However, your DSLR footage may be part of a bigger project, which was shot interlaced.

▲ The settings you used when shooting are likely the settings you should use when creating a sequence.

CROSSING THE STREAMS

It is generally not recommended to mix frame rates, but sometimes you have to. Set your sequence for 29.97 and drop in the 24p material. Final Cut Pro X will blend the frames to smooth out the image.

A good place to check your footage is in the Inspector. Simply select a clip in your event that is representative of the project. You can then click the Info button in the Inspector (if the Inspector is closed, just press Command+4 to open it).

Creating a New Project

By creating a Final Cut Pro project, you will have a file that tracks the editing decisions you make as well as which media you choose to include. Each project you create will have a single sequence in the Timeline panel.

Here's how to create your project.

1. Do *one* of the following:
   › In Final Cut Pro, choose File > New Project (or press Command+N).
   › In the Project Library click the New Project button.

   A new sheet opens.

2. Enter a descriptive name for the new project.

3. Specify a default event for the project using the menu.

   The default event is used to hold any media that's dragged from the Finder into the project's Timeline.

4. Set the starting timecode for the project. The default is 00:00:00:00.

   The most common starting point is 01:00:00:00 (also known as one hour). These numbers break down as follows, hours : minutes : seconds : frames.

DRAGGING TO THE TIMELINE
We don't typically recommend dragging media directly into the Timeline. We strongly recommend that you take the time to target the correct event to hold your footage.

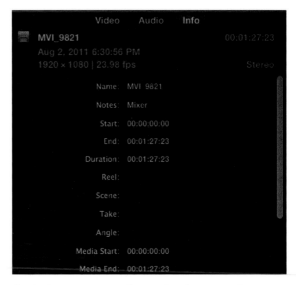

▲ The Inspector can tell you a lot about your footage. Click the Info button to see details on frame size and frame rate.

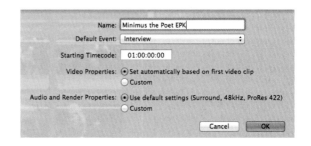

WHAT IS DROP FRAME TIMECODE?
If you've selected a frame rate of 29.97 or 59.94 fps, you have the option to use drop frame timecode. The standard drop frame used most often is where frame numbers 0 and 1 are skipped occasionally to maintain the consistent fractional frame rates that match actual running time. This is the standard for broadcast television, which really isn't 30 frames a second. Frames are counted differently (not truly dropped) to make sure that a one-hour program is precisely one hour in length. Think of drop frame as being like leap years. You don't lose any days and the earth doesn't move faster, but the calendar stays accurate. Drop frame timecode is the correct option for most projects, although you may be asked to use non-drop frame timecode for corporate video projects. In this case, the timecode counter counts at a consistent rate without dropping any numbers from the count.

Defining Video Properties

Now that you've set the descriptive details for the project you'll need to set the technical aspects for the project. The first area to resolve is the video properties. You can either match the first clip or manually adjust the video properties. You have two options:

> **Set automatically based on first video clip.** This option automatically conforms the sequence to the first clip that you drag into it. This is the default value and works on the assumption that the way you shot the footage is the way you want to edit it. Just be certain that you drag in a clip that represents your project.

> **Custom.** The Custom menu supports several formats, including standard definition and high definition video as well as 2K and 4K for digital cinema workflows. The Resolution and Rate menus adjust their choices based on the Format you choose.

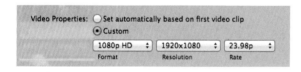

We believe that you should *actually know* which sequence settings you are using. As discussed earlier, always examine your footage and use the Inspector or List view to determine the predominant format you are editing. For this DSLR project, we used 1080p | 1920 x 1080 | 23.98p.

Defining Audio and Render Properties

You next need to customize your Audio and Render properties. The default option is to render all files to Apple ProRes 422 with the Audio Channels set to Surround Sound mix at 48 kHz.

These default settings work well for most cases, but we prefer a slight tweak. Click the Custom radio button and set the Audio Channels menu to Stereo. This will ensure broader compatibility for your file when it's viewed over the Internet or on portable media players. The other properties are fine as is, unless your client has requested a higher-quality video codec or audio sampling rate.

Review your settings once more, and then click OK. The new project opens in the Timeline.

▲ Switch your Audio Channels setting to Stereo (unless you have to deliver in surround sound).

Understanding the Project Library

The Project Library is where you organize your individual projects. When you create a new project, the Project Library lets you specify where to store it (you can also relocate it later). It also lets you seamlessly switch from one project to another in just a few clicks.

As you progress through editing (and the rest of this book), you'll find that we keep coming back to the Project Library. For now, we'll focus on creating, modifying, and moving projects. Later in the book you'll tackle tasks like media management and publishing.

Modifying a Project Before Editing

The easiest time to edit a project is before you edit any media into it. Once a clip has been inserted into a project, its frame rate is locked. This means that if you start at 24 fps, you cannot change your mind down the road and make it 29.97. Additionally, cutting footage into the wrong-sized sequence can result in unintentional changes to a frame's size.

BACK UP A PROJECT
If you need to back up a project, just open the Project Library. You can then drag a project onto a new drive to copy it. You'll have the choice of duplicating the project as well as including all referenced events or clips.

▲ When you drag between drives, be sure to hold down the Command key to move the project (as opposed to copying it). If you see a plus symbol, the project is being copied; just the project name highlighted (as shown here) is a move.

Before you start editing a sequence, it's a good idea to look through it closely. To really check a project's properties in detail, you'll need two panels visible:

> **Inspector.** If it's not visible, press Command+4 to show the Inspector.

> **Project Library.** If the Project Library isn't open, click the Project Library button at the bottom-left corner of the Final Cut Pro main window.

With both open, you can now control your project.

1. Confirm which drive you want to hold the project.

   Although the system boot drive is a logical choice, you'll find that it's not always ideal. Many render files will be added to the project folder as you build effects and color correct. As such, you can quickly slow down your operating system drive. This method also makes it difficult to move the project from machine to machine.

   We favor putting the project onto the same drive as the events, using the drive- or partition-per-client approach we discussed earlier. When doing this, however, it is essential that you periodically back up your project.

2. Hold down the Command key and drag your project to a new drive to move it.

3. Choose the Move Project Only option and click OK.

4. Select the project on the new drive by clicking it once.

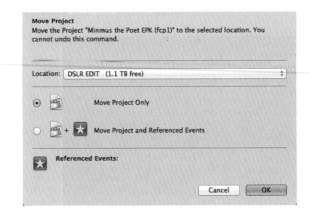

5. Examine the Properties Inspector and determine if you want to change any properties. To modify the project, just click the Project Properties button (shaped like a wrench).

6. In the Notes field in the Properties Inspector you can add any relevant project information.

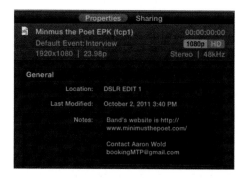

7. When you're ready to use a project, double-click on the project in the Project Library. The project opens into a Timeline view.

 GOT A SAN? USE IT
If your computer is attached to a high-speed storage area network (SAN), you can use it to edit video. You can store projects and events on a SAN location. This can make it easier to move a project from computer to computer in your office as needed.

Organizing the Project Library with Folders

As the number of projects you build increases, a little organization can go a long way. Chances are you use folders on your computer to organize files. Perhaps you have folders for different clients or jobs in your Documents folder. Well, the same logic applies here. Remember that it's never too late to get organized. You can rename, copy, or move your projects when necessary.

1. If the Project Library is not visible, press Command+O or click the Project Library button at the bottom-left corner of the Final Cut Pro main window.

2. Select the disk (or existing folder) that you want to add a folder to by clicking it once.

3. Click the New Folder button at the bottom-left corner of the Final Cut Pro main window.

An empty folder called New Folder appears on the disk or in the folder you selected.

4. Give the folder a descriptive name by typing it and pressing Return.

5. Drag a project onto the folder to place it inside.

6. You can open or close the folder by clicking the disclosure triangle to the left of the folder name.

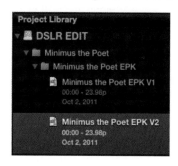

Keep in mind that you can use as many folders as needed. In fact, you can place folders inside other folders for additional organization. We typically create a parent folder with the client's name. We'll then use embedded folders within the parent folder to keep track of each major element (such as Electronic Press Kit, Concert Film, Music Video, etc.). By using folders, you can easily keep track of different versions of a project as you incorporate client feedback and move through the creative editing process. It is not uncommon to have several versions of a project that all reference the same event.

▲ You can preview a project from within the Project Library without even opening it.

▲ If you Control-click an active Timeline History button, you can see a list of recently opened projects.

Previewing a Project

As your library grows, you'll end up with several projects. Although accurate project names help organize the Project Library, Final Cut Pro X provides two options that you can use to preview your project without actually opening the project.

1. Select a project in your Project Library.

   The project loads into the Viewer

2. Use *one* of these methods to preview the project:

   › Move the pointer over the filmstrip to skim the project. Move the mouse to the right and left to see the footage update.

   › Press the spacebar to play the project forward from the current skimmer position (the pink vertical line). Press the spacebar again to stop playback.

3. Double-click a project when you're ready to open it.

Switching Projects

As you work in Final Cut Pro X, you may find that you open and close several projects while working. Perhaps it's to check the settings used in another project, to check how an effect was built, or to copy some media and move it to another sequence. Whatever the reason, it's easy to switch between recently used projects:

› You can click the Go back in Timeline History or Go forward in Timeline History buttons to switch between your last used projects.

› If you want to see a list of recently opened projects, Control-click and hold on one of the active arrows. A list of projects opened during your editing session appears.

Duplicating a Project

As you work with a project, you may reach a point when it is a good idea to duplicate your current project. For example, you might want to significantly experiment with an edit while preserving a point of reference to jump back to. You may also need to revise or update a completed project to make a new version.

Here's how to duplicate a project.

1. Select a project in your Project Library.

2. Choose File > Duplicate or press Command+D.

3. In the new dialog that opens, choose a location for the duplicated project.

4. Use the radio buttons to choose whether to duplicate the project only or to include referenced events or used clips only.

   If you want to move the project to another drive for portability, choose one of the media options. The referenced events option is a good choice if you are in the middle of a project and you want to preserve options. The used clips only option works best to archive a completed project. You'll explore both of these in greater detail in Chapter 11.

5. Choose whether you want to include render files.

   The duplicate project may need to rerender certain files in your Timeline if you leave this option deselected. However, the benefit of rerendering is that you will get fresh renders of only what is needed. If you're working on a fast computer, the need to render may be greatly reduced because files can play in real time.

Deleting a Project

If you decide that you no longer need a project, you can remove it. Deleting a project removes it from your drive. However, your media is not deleted because it is stored separately in events.

1. Select a project in your Project Library.

2. Choose File > Move Project to Trash (or press Command+Delete).

   The project is moved from your Project Library into the Finder Trash.

3. To permanently delete the project, switch to the Finder. Choose Finder > Empty Trash.

   Once the trash is emptied, you cannot restore a project. Be sure you have backed up any projects you want to keep before you discard a project. For more on media management, see Chapter 11.

▲ Be sure to consider which aspects of your project you want to include when you duplicate it.

CHAPTER **6**

Syncing Footage

We love our DSLR cameras and the beautiful footage they help us shoot, but there's one thing we hate—the audio. The audio recording capabilities of a DSLR camera out of the box would be outperformed by taking two cans and stretching a string between them. Your cell phone has a better microphone than your DSLR.

So although you're anxious to start editing, you have one more task in front of you before you begin editing your program—sound syncing. You might be thinking, "Why worry about that now? Surely that can happen while I'm editing my show." The answer is not really. A little work now will help you to avoid a lot of work later.

▲ One benefit of a dual-system sound approach is that the recorders let you properly monitor while recording. Be sure to invest in a good pair of headphones as well (iPod earbuds don't cut it).

▲ The nightclub had a lot of ambient sound, so the only way to capture the performance was to connect the external audio recorder to the house mixing board. Each camera used a reference mic for syncing sound.

Dual-System Sound Revisited

We explored the dual-system (or sync sound) workflows back in Chapter 1, "Shooting with Editing in Mind." (You did read Chapter 1 and not just skip to this chapter, right?) You learned that the microphone built into your DSLR is "OK" at best. It's fine to use in a pinch and it's OK for background sound, but it's abysmal when it comes to interviews or critical audio. The camera mic's best use is to provide good reference audio to sync up to the real audio you record with a stand-alone audio recorder.

 DON'T HAVE SYNC SOUND?
If you recorded your audio directly into your camera with an on-camera microphone or you used an audio bridge, you may want to skip this chapter, but you'll eventually need this information and could continue to read on and learn a thing or two.

Hopefully when you shot dual-system sound (DSS), you got as clean audio on your DSLR as possible. The reason is that Final Cut Pro X can automatically sync your two sources based on the audio waveform in each source. So if you have no sound (or very low-quality sound) from your camera mic, this becomes nearly impossible. Trust us; you don't want to have to sync your footage manually because it can be quite time-consuming and rather frustrating (if not impossible).

Here are a few audio reminders, because we have learned that when it comes to audio tips, repetition means eventual success:

> Don't talk or hum while shooting to keep your camera audio as clean as possible.

> Don't block the mic. We've seen people who have accidentally put tape or even their fingers over the pinhole mic and recorded no sound.

> Make sure you haven't disabled the camera audio.

> If you plug in an on-camera mic, make sure it's powered on and working. Again, if your on-camera mic is not working, you end up with silent video that requires manual syncing.

> Remember that for most DSLR cameras there is no way to listen to your in-camera audio while recording. Your best bet is to roll a few seconds and play the clip back to confirm you are getting sound.

> When it comes to audio, there is no such thing as being too paranoid.

Syncing Audio and Video

Final Cut Pro has the ability to automatically analyze two (or more) clips and sync them up based on their audio. This is of course useful when recording DSS but can also be used if you are shooting with two or more cameras and want to sync them up. Although Final Cut Pro X has not released its multicam editing feature (as of this writing), we have found a workaround that will allow you to more easily edit multiple camera angles in the same project. There are two ways to sync your audio: automatically within Final Cut Pro X or by using markers. Let's explore both.

Syncing Clips Automatically

The easiest way to sync is to let Final Cut Pro X try to do it automatically. As long as you have sufficient levels in your reference audio, the process is successful most of the time. The process works best when you need to sync a single video file to a single audio file. Here's how it works.

1. Select an audio clip and a video clip in the Event Browser.

   You can select multiple clips by holding down the Command key and clicking on each clip. You'll know a clip is selected when a yellow selection box appears around the edge of each clip.

COMPOUND: 7 VS. X

In previous versions of Final Cut Pro a compound clip would be a lot like a nested clip—clips inside of clips. In Final Cut Pro X it is simply a new clip made up of two or more clips.

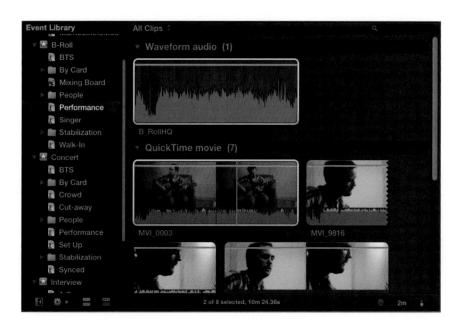

2. Choose Clip > Synchronize Clips (Option+ Command+G.)

   A new clip is created in the Event Browser. This new clip is a compound clip, which means it is a clip made up of at least two other clips.

3. Look for a new clip in the Event Browser.

   Newly synced clips do not have any keywords attached. If you're filtering your Event Browser using a Keyword Collection, you might not see the new clip. Be sure to switch your view to see all clips in the Event Browser. You might want to tag the synced clip with additional keywords.

Depending on the size of the original files, this new clip could appear very quickly or take a while. If you can't find the clip, simply select the search box in the upper-right corner of the Event Library and type in **synchronized clip**. You'll probably find it after you type **synch**.

4. Select the clip in the Event Browser and click the Play button.

5. Watch the clip play back and check for sync.

   You should hear the reference audio and the DSS play back. Later you'll learn how to discard the audio.

I SYNCED, BUT IT DIDN'T WORK

Sometimes the automatic sync command takes time (especially with long clips or bad audio). Make sure you click the Dashboard and open the Background Tasks window. If the syncing task is still running, your audio is likely out of sync.

What Order Does Final Cut Pro X Use When Synchronizing Clips?

It's important to know how Final Cut Pro analyzes the clips for sync points. After all, there are several ways to create sync: manually inserted markers, timecode, file creation date, and even audio content.

Here's the order of operations:

1. If Final Cut Pro X can't immediately find sync points, the clips are synced at their respective starting points.

2. The syncing is then refined by a background process.

3. Final Cut Pro will try to use audio waveforms to sync up your footage.

4. It that does not work, Final Cut Pro X will look for markers.

The good news is that you really do have options and backup methods.

◀ If you look at the figure closely, you'll see that the reference and the sync sound's waveforms closely match.

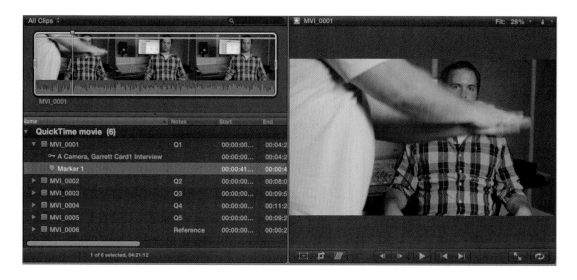

Syncing with Markers

If auto syncing fails, there's always the manual method. Let's suppose you forgot to record audio on your DSLR. Perhaps the mic's battery died halfway through the shoot. You are *not* out of luck. You can still sync your audio and video clips using markers. Essentially, you can place markers on two points that you determine will match (such as the closing of the clapboard to the spike in the audio track).

To use this method, you need to put a marker on each clip that you want to synchronize.

1. Select the video clip that you want to synchronize.

2. Using the skimmer or the playhead and viewer, scrub through the clip until you find the frame where you slapped the clapboard closed (or clapped your hands).

   You should be able to see it in the clip.

3. Press the M key to place a marker into the clip.

4. Repeat the process for the audio clip. Once you find this spot, press the M key to place a marker at that point.

5. With both markers set, you can choose Clip > Synchronize Clips (Option+Command+G). A new clip is created.

   Remember to select the clip and relabel it with a more descriptive name.

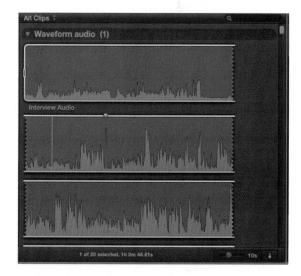

▲ It might be easier to spot the audio sync point when viewing the clip in Filmstrip view. You can use your J-K-L or arrow keys for finer navigation.

 **ZOOM ZOOM**

When placing a marker on a clip, it's often easiest to view the clip in Filmstrip view. You can then zoom all the way in by pressing Command+=. If you need to navigate a clip, you can step through a clip using the J-K-L keys (or even the left and right arrow keys to find the perfect spot).

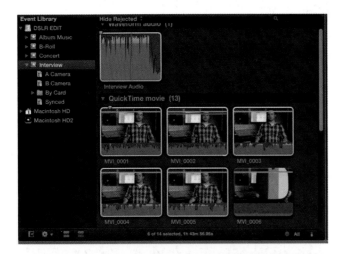

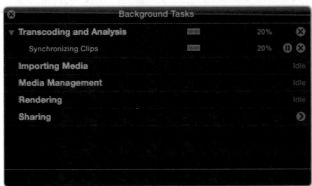

▲ You can select a single audio track and multiple video clips when syncing an interview.

Syncing Interviews Automatically

When we record interviews, we tend to start and stop the camera periodically because of the technical limitations of record length. However, we tend to leave the audio rolling. This isn't laziness; it's just that we've been burned by thinking the audio recorder was rolling when it wasn't. (Oh, you have to push the Record button twice?) What we do, however, is make sure to give the clip a sync point with each new video take. This can be a full clapboard or just your voice calling out the clip number with a sharp clap of your hands.

Fortunately, Final Cut Pro can automatically analyze and sync the audio and video clips in your project using auto-synchronization. In our example, we had five video files for the groups of questions and one audio track. You can tell Final Cut Pro to analyze and sync the clips together into a compound clip in the Event Browser.

Here's how to sync a long interview.

1. Select the audio clip for your interview in the Event Browser.

BOY THOSE FANS ARE RUNNING LOUDLY
The process of syncing clips is very CPU intensive. In this case we're syncing five video tracks to a nearly hour-long audio track. The syncing can slow down your computer significantly. It's a good idea to sync long clips before a lunch break or at the end of a workday.

2. Hold down the Command key and click to select the video clips you want to sync.

3. Choose Clip > Synchronize Clips (Command+Option+G).

4. Check the Background Tasks window for progress.

   If you see a hollow circle in the lower-left corner of a clip, it is still being processed.

5. Locate the new clip in your Event Browser.

   Synced compound clips are labeled with the additional text "synchronized clip" in the Event Browser. The original clips are not affected.

In this case Final Cut Pro syncs by using the audio content. If that were to fail, the solution would be to add a marker into the audio file at each point when the hand clap spiked. You'd then add markers into each video clip on the hand claps as well.

Syncing Multiple Cameras

Although it's not officially supported (as of this writing), Final Cut Pro X can sync multiple video clips into a single, lined-up, compound clip. This is a great workaround if you need to do multicamera editing.

Just as before, the best way to line up your footage is to make sure you have the best reference audio on each of your DSLRs and your replacement track from your external audio recorder. Instead of selecting just two clips in an event, select all the clips from the shoot that belong together. Don't throw in any random or really distorted media because it will throw off Final Cut Pro's syncing algorithm.

When shooting, it's best to keep all of your cameras running continuously, because this will make syncing easier. For example, we shot the Minimus the Poet

▲ Make sure your camera operators are in agreement as to when to cut a take during a musical performance or live event. We typically stop and start a clip in between songs.

concert using five angles. We started and stopped the cameras between each song so we could have a clean clip per song. The audio, on the other hand, was recorded for the whole concert to a Zoom H4N that was plugged into the soundboard of the venue for a clean track.

This workflow is needed for DSLRs because you have to restart your cameras during the shoot due to clip length limits (ranging from 5–20 minutes depending on the manufacturer). Don't panic; Final Cut Pro X has the ability to line up multiple clips into the same synchronized compound clip. You just need to be patient because this could take some time.

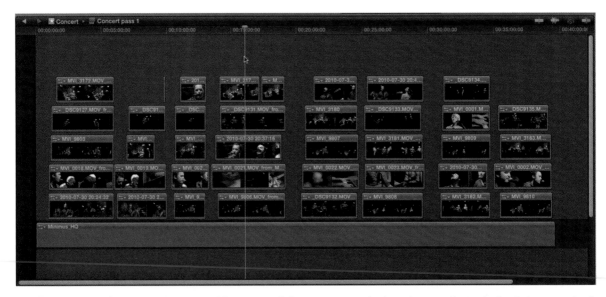

▲ Although it took some time, we were able to sync all five cameras to the hour-long audio track. Apple has promised true multicam editing in the next version of Final Cut Pro X.

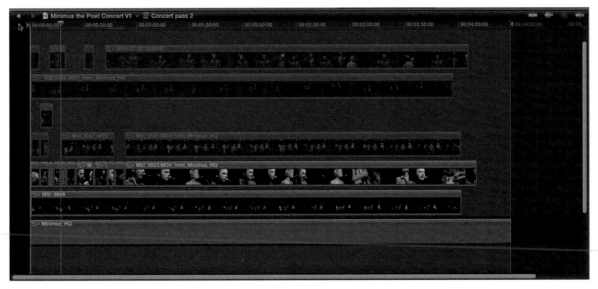

▲ While you wait for true multicamera editing, you can step into the compound clip and use the Blade tool to cut apart tracks and pull your selects together. You can then delete or toggle the visibility of the unwanted clips.

In our tests we threw more than 80 clips from five cameras at Final Cut Pro, and the audio track was about an hour long. Even though it took a while (about 2 hours on a MacBook Pro), it did work. We were able to track progress using the Background Tasks window.

Turning Off the Bad Tracks

If you play through your newly created synced clip now, you'll notice the joy of great DSS audio (and the despair of those fuzzy echoing tracks that were recorded by your DSLR). The last task you need to do before you start to edit with these tracks is to turn off those less-than-stellar audio tracks.

Here's how to use only the best audio.

1. Select a newly synced (compound) clip in your Event Library.

2. Open the Inspector panel.

   You can open the Inspector panel by clicking the small blue *i* symbol in the toolbar. You can also press Command+4.

3. If it is not already selected, switch to the Audio inspector by clicking the Audio tab (the middle button at the top of the Inspector).

4. Locate the Channel Configuration section.

   You may have to scroll down in the Audio inspector to see it.

5. Locate the audio channels from all the clips that Final Cut Pro X has synced in this compound clip.

   If you don't see a list of clips that make up the compound clip below Channel Configuration, click the disclosure triangle to the left of the words Channels: Stereo.

6. Now comes the fun part; you can simply deselect and turn off any tracks you do not want to hear.

   Most likely, you will turn off all your camera tracks except for the clean DSS audio recording.

Those camera reference tracks can still be used. If you think you may want to grab ambient sound off any of the DSLR sources, you can leave them active and lower the volume of those clips during your edit. For example, although our sync sound for the concert sounds great, mixing in a little of the crowd noise from the camera microphone helps re-create the sound of the live event. Remember that this is all nondestructive, so you can turn off tracks now and then go back and turn them on later as needed.

▲ After syncing sound, you'll likely want to disable the original audio (the reference sound) and only leave the higher quality sync sound active.

Creating Smart Collections of Synced Footage

Back in Chapter 4, "Organizing Your Media," you learned about Smart Collections. This is a perfect time to revisit that technology. You can make a Smart Collection for all of your synchronized clips so that they're easier to find.

Here's how to save time with a Smart Collection.

1. Type **synchronized** into the Search field to filter your view and only see synchronized clips.

2. Click the Filter button (the small magnifying glass to the left of the search field). The Filter window appears.

3. Click the New Smart Collection button to create a Smart Collection. A new Smart Collection icon labeled "Untitled" will appear to the left in the Event Library.

4. Select the new Smart Collection and give it a proper name, such as **Synchronized Clips**.

If you want that same Smart Collection to work in a variety of your events, simply copy the purple icon into another event. For example, in this project we've synchronized clips for the Interview, an acoustic performance in our B-Roll event, and of course the main Concert. Simply drag the Smart Collection to a new event and a copy of all the Smart Collection's parameters

will appear and sort the media in that event by the rules you set up.

Remember that you can make your Smart Collections even smarter by adding additional criteria. To modify a Smart Collection, simply double-click its icon. For example, we could create a Smart Collection of only synchronized clips that were interviews but not concert footage. In the Filter panel you can click the plus (+) menu in the upper-right corner of the window and select "keywords." From there you can select which keywords you want Final Cut Pro X to refine the Smart Collection by. You could also create effective criteria using Shoot Date or Roles to help you limit the filter. As you can see, you can create a variety of Smart Collections for all of your synced footage, making it easier to find when needed.

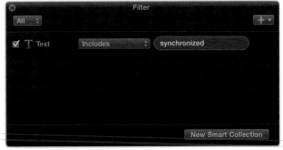

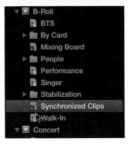

◀ By using the Filter commands, you can create a new Smart Collection to make it easier to find your synchronized clips.

I KEEP TRYING, BUT FINAL CUT PRO X WON'T LET ME CREATE A SMART COLLECTION

Here's the problem. You've brilliantly created a Smart Collection that refines your footage to precisely the media you want. You choose Create Smart Collection, but then you see a mysterious dialog that shows, "The operation could not be completed. When creating a Smart Collection, you must have an event selected, not a hard drive location. The reason is that Final Cut Pro does not know which Event Library to attach the Smart Collection to. So select an event and try again. Voilà. No mystery dialog.

Syncing with DualEyes

Another great way to sync your footage is with a stand-alone, third-party application called DualEyes from Singular Software (www.singularsoftware.com/dualeyes.html). What's really cool is that DualEyes can sync your DSLR video clips and your separate high-quality audio recordings before you import them into Final Cut Pro X, avoiding the hassle of creating compound clips and then having to disable the poor-quality audio channels. It creates a new video clip containing the good audio married to the original video, so there is no loss in video quality. Plus, your original files remain untouched on your drive. In our tests, DualEyes was significantly faster than Final Cut Pro X (but it will set you back $149).

Here is a quick overview of how DualEyes works.

1. Launch the DualEyes application.

2. Click the New Project button.

3. Give the project a descriptive name, and select a location where you want to save the project. We suggest saving in a media folder related to the project you are syncing because DualEyes does create new media and temp files when it runs. The application also generates a report file that you can peruse to determine any problem clips.

4. Drag in the video and audio files that you want to sync or click the Add Media button (the plus symbol).

   Officially, you can add multiple video files, but it is best to stick with only one good audio file. This is not multicamera prep, so you should only put video in from one camera or camera angle. Don't throw everything in at once. With that said, we dumped in the sound track from our concert and every video angle (even a few random clips), and it did an excellent job of matching the sound.

5. Click the Options menu and choose from the following options:

   > **Replace Audio for MOV and AVI files.** DualEyes will create a new file that contains the video from the original clip and the synced audio for MOV and AVI files. Make sure you select this option, or you won't get a new self-contained movie file with clean audio.

   > **Correct Drift.** Cameras can record at 24P, 29.97i, and so on. Audio devices like to keep rates at 30 frames per second. These timing differences between the audio and video can sometimes cause drift, which means audio and video could be perfectly synced in one segment of the video but unsynced in a different segment. The Correct Drift option corrects this so that everything is in sync all the time. This problem tends to show up in very long recordings.

   > **Level Audio:** Before DualEyes, the creator of the software had a great product used by podcasters worldwide called the Levelator. This product did a wonderful job of smoothing out variations in sound. Well, that's built into DualEyes. If your audio levels vary a lot between clips, Dual-Eyes can normalize the audio levels. If you've recorded from a professional soundboard at a venue, this might be overkill, but for interviews and most other situations, it works great. It's almost always safe to use this option, but it will take a bit longer to process.

6. Click the scissors button to start synchronizing clips.

7. You can monitor progress within the app and view the Output column to track progress.

   When it's done, you will see a new clip that contains the good audio and the good video (minus the bad audio). You will find this movie in the same folder as the original movie with the bad audio. Its name will be appended with "_from_" and then the name of the good audio file you referenced.

8. Simply import it into Final Cut Pro X, and you are good to go.

DualEyes is a popular choice with those who need to prepare footage to hand off to clients or other team members. It's popular because it's fast and it saves several steps at the editing stage (which often get screwed up due to poor communication). We recommend you download the free demo and try it out.

Editing Essentials

At this point you should have created events for your project, imported and organized your media with keywords and into Smart Collections, and marked clips as favorites and rejected. Everything is now organized. You have created a place for everything and everything is in its place. It's time to start editing your project. The first task you need to do is select your first shot (this will set all of the parameters for the sequence that's created). There is no need to overthink. Remember that with nonlinear editing you can easily replace a shot or rearrange the order of your program with a simple drag and drop. Think of video editing like word processing except that you're using video and audio files.

Over the next few chapters, we'll cut together a short promotional video for a band called Minimus the Poet. It will consist of an on-camera interview and some concert footage. Of course, you should already be familiar with this footage because you learned how to import, tag, and organize it in Chapters 3 and 4. Now all that hard work is going to pay off, and the editing can begin.

Selecting Clips and Ranges

In Chapter 4, "Organizing Your Media," you performed tasks like viewing clips in List view or Filmstrip view. You also learned how to skim through a clip to select an area to which you wanted to add keywords. You're about to revisit those same skills but with a slightly different purpose. Now that it's time to edit, you'll need to actually choose the parts of the clips you want to use in your project. These may be the favorites you marked earlier or new selections based on your video's story and pacing.

Working with Selections

A selection allows you to specify which portions of a clip you want to use in a project. For example, you can choose to set an In point when the interviewee starts answering a relevant question and an Out point when the answer is finished. This essentially cuts out the voice of the interviewer asking the question and any chatter at the end, such as, "Was that okay?"

Take the time to precisely select the best part of a clip before you add it to the Timeline. It keeps your Timeline neat and will reduce the need for additional editing time down the road.

WHAT SHOULD I CUT FIRST?
When creating a video, you may be tempted to start with the most exciting footage to get a viewer's attention (in our case that would be the concert footage). The reality is that the narrative portion is often the most essential part. For this video, the real story will come from the interview. The best approach is to cut the sound bites together first. The story can then be enhanced with concert footage, b-roll, and performance shots that are interspersed throughout the story.

Working with Filmstrips

The first step to editing a clip is to select the frames you want to use. The first step in selecting frames is to switch to properly viewing the clip in the Event Browser. We find that working in Filmstrip view is easiest when it comes time to start editing. The major benefit is that you can quickly skim through a bunch of clips and choose the usable or desirable portions. Here is a quick overview of the two different views:

> **Filmstrip view.** Displays the clips as a series of thumbnail images. Filmstrip view is useful when you want to visually locate your clips quickly.

> **List view.** Displays a list of your clips with associated file information. In this view you can view or sort clips by data such as duration, creation date, rating, keyword, and so on. You can also click on a clip's disclosure triangle and reveal any keywords associated with the clip.

So should you view clips in Filmstrip view or List view? Well, there is no right answer. You will probably jump back and forth between both views as you edit. We usually need to jump back to List view to organize or locate clips from time to time. However, Filmstrip view makes the act of selecting a range much easier. You can easily jump back and forth between these views by clicking the "Show clips in filmstrip view" button (Command+Option+1) or "Show clips in list view" button (Command+Option+2).

HOW MANY FRAMES ARE SHOWN?
Adjusting the Duration slider expands and contracts the amount of detail shown in each clip's filmstrip. The longer the duration of each thumbnail, the fewer thumbnails each clip displays, and the more clips are displayed in the Event Browser.

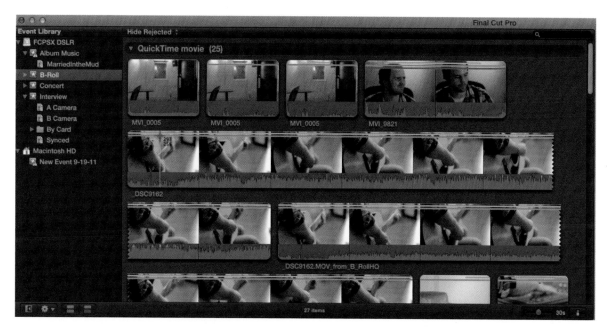

▲ The Filmstrip view lets you see each clip as its own thumbnail. This can help when browsing visually.

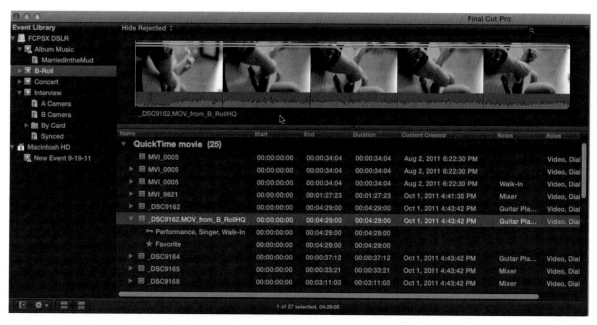

▲ The List view is very efficient as it lets you see several columns of information about your clips.

To make the filmstrips easier to work with, here are a few useful tips. Once you have used these three shortcuts, you will probably never touch the Zoom slider again:

> Adjust the Duration in the bottom-right corner of the Event Browser to show All. You can then quickly see more of your clips simultaneously. Press Shift+Z to set the Duration slider to All, which displays an image for each clip.

> When you decide on the clip you want to work with, simply select it and zoom in to the necessary detail. We've found that the slider can be a bit finicky. Using keyboards shortcuts here can prevent a few gray hairs.

> To zoom in and see greater detail, press Command+= (equals).

> To zoom out and show you less detail (but more clip), press Command+- (minus).

Selecting an Entire Clip

If you want to use an entire clip, that's easy; just select it. The easiest way to do this (whether the clip is in an event or the Timeline) is to just click the clip once. You'll know that a clip is actively selected when a yellow border appears around the clip.

HOW LONG IS MY CLIP?
After you select a clip, just press Control+D. The timecode numbers in the center of the Dashboard will update and show you the duration for the selected clip.

Some editors prefer the workflow of selecting an entire clip to edit and then bringing it into the Timeline. They then trim the parts of the clip they do not want to use from the Timeline using the Blade tool or by grabbing the edge of a clip and dragging left or right.

Although selecting an entire clip is very fast, we don't recommend it because it means more work in the Timeline. Usually, you would only select the entire clip if you already refined it on import or if you've used keywords to reject material you know you won't use.

If you've carefully created your clips, you can also select multiple clips to edit. In this case there are some useful shortcuts to select multiple clips in the Event Browser or the Timeline:

> **To select a contiguous, linear series of clips.** Click the first clip, and then Shift-click the last clip. This will select all the clips in the range.

> **To select a number of individual clips.** Click the first clip, and then Command-click remaining clips. This will let you choose multiple clips in an event or Timeline that you want to select.

> **To select all clips in the Event Browser or the Timeline.** Click to select a panel and choose Edit > Select All (or press Command+A).

> **To select multiple clips by dragging.** Click and drag a selection rectangle over the Timeline or event to choose the desired clips.

If needed, you can also deselect clips. Just click a different clip or click in an empty area of the Event Browser or the Timeline. If you've selected a range of clips, you can also Command-click on a clip to remove it from the selected range. The keyboard shortcut Command+Shift+A deselects all clips.

Selecting a Range

Although selecting an entire clip is useful, more often you will be selecting a range (or part of a clip) that you want to bring into your project. The best way to think of this is like cropping. Selecting exactly a part of an image—or in this case a clip—that you want your viewer to focus on. There are several ways to do this, and you will probably use more than one.

SELECTING A RANGE IN THE EVENT BROWSER

The most frequent location for selecting a range is the Event Browser. Here's how to choose just the part of a clip that you want to use.

1. Click a clip to first select it (you'll see the yellow selection border).

2. Drag the yellow bars at the beginning and end of the clip. Drag until you see the start and stop frames that you want to use.

An even quicker way to select a range is to use In and Out points. This method works well when combined with skimming.

1. Place the skimmer over a desired clip. You can just hover over the clip; there's no need to click.

2. Skim left or right to see the clip play back. If skimming is turned off, just press S to turn on skimming.

3. When you see the frame you want to start with, press the I key to mark an In point.

4. Skim to where you want to the clip to end, and press the O key to mark an Out point.

   You'll notice that the yellow bounding box surrounds only the precise part of the clip that you want to work with.

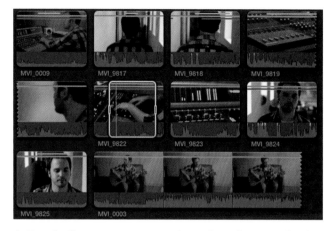

▲ By selecting a range, you can choose just what part of a clip you want to use.

![check icon] **DEALING WITH ACCIDENTAL SELECTIONS**
Sometimes when you click on a clip, you'll accidentally select the whole clip when all you want to do is grab a range in the middle. Instead of deselecting the clip and then reselecting the section you want, hold down the Option key. You can immediately drag to grab a smaller selection. (This function only works in the Event Browser, not in the Timeline.)

Using Filters and Favorites to Make Selections

In Chapter 4 you learned a lot about using keywords and favorites. These organization methods are a great way to quickly select a clip or a range for use as a selection. The Filter menu in the Event Library offers several ways to change what is displayed. Click the Filter menu at the top of the Event Browser, and choose one of these options:

› **All Clips.** Shows all clips in the event.

› **Hide Rejected.** Shows all clips or range selections *except* those you've rated Reject.

› **No Ratings or Keywords.** Shows only the clips or range selections without ratings or keywords.

› **Favorites.** Shows only the clips or range selections you've rated Favorite. Also, if you click on the green bar on the filmstrip (which indicates a favorite range), that favorite will set a range automatically.

› **Rejected.** Shows only the clips or range selections you've rated Reject.

SELECTING A RANGE IN THE TIMELINE

Although you haven't edited clips into a Timeline yet (that comes soon), let's jump forward a bit. Often, you'll want to make a selection to a clip after it's been edited into a Timeline. You might select a range in your Timeline to delete a portion of a clip or to select several contiguous clips in your Timeline. This is useful for tasks like moving, filtering, or making selective adjustments to things like audio.

There are multiple ways to select a range in the Timeline:

> In the Timeline, choose Range Selection from the Tools menu (or press R). You can then drag to select a range.

> You can use the I and O keys to set the selection start and end points. To clear an In and Out point, hold down the Option key and press I or O to clear the In or Out (respectively), or press Option+X to clear both.

> You can place the skimmer over a clip to select it and press X to mark the entire clip below the skimmer.

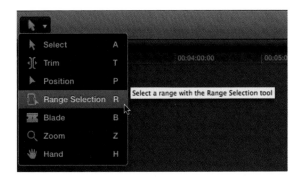

▲ The Range Selection tool is a useful way to drag and select a range of clips in your Timeline. You may want to select several clips in order to move or filter them.

Adding to and Removing Clips from the Timeline

The good news about Final Cut Pro X is that there are two or three ways to do almost every task. The bad news about Final Cut Pro X is that there are two or three ways to do almost every task.

Our advice is learn and try each method, but ultimately choose the way that works for you and stick to it. This advice is particularly true when adding clips to the Timeline. You can use keyboard shortcuts or menus, or simply drag a clip where you want it to go.

Three Essential Types of Edits

Although there are many ways to edit, Final Cut Pro X offers three basic editing commands. You'll use these three basic commands extensively when editing in the Timeline:

> **Append a clip to your project.** The most common edit you'll make is an Append to End edit. This edit just places the clip (or clip range) you've selected in your Event Browser after the last clip in your Timeline.

> **Insert a clip into your project.** An Insert edit does exactly what its name implies; it can insert a clip between two existing clips or even in the middle of one clip by splitting it into two parts. When using an Insert edit, your program's duration gets longer.

> **Connect a clip to your project.** The third basic edit is the Connect edit. Final Cut Pro X is unique in that you can attach a clip on a layer above an existing clip, connecting them at a single point. You can even attach multiple clips to the main clip on your Timeline. If you move the main clip, the attached (or connected) clips move right along with it, keeping everything lined up and in sync.

APPEND TO END EDIT

An easy way to think about the Append to End edit command is that it adds clips to the end of your Timeline and extends the length of your program. This command can be used by dragging media into the Timeline or by using the keyboard.

Here's how to make an Append edit.

1. Select a clip (or multiple clips) in the Event Browser.

2. Click the Append button in the toolbar (or press E) to add the selected clip(s) to the end of the Timeline.

3. You can alternately drag media from the Event Browser toward the end of the Timeline. No matter where you let go, it will snap to the very end of the Timeline into the center dark gray area. From now on we will refer to this area as the *primary storyline*.

INSERT EDIT

You can also perform an Insert edit into your primary storyline by dragging. The trick here is that you need to drag the clip you want to insert and drop it in between two existing clips. The problem with dragging clips to perform an Insert edit is that you need to be fairly precise. Using a keyboard shortcut is not only easier, but also more accurate. Here is a much more robust workflow.

To make an Insert edit, follow these steps.

1. Select one or more clips in the Event Browser.

2. Move the playhead (or skimmer) to the primary storyline where you want to insert the clip.

   This can be between clips, or you can cut a clip in half. You can press the I key to mark an In point if you want to be precise.

3. Click the Insert button in the toolbar (or press W) to insert the selected clip(s) to the specified point in the Timeline.

   The clips are then added to the Timeline. Any clips after the insertion point are automatically pushed forward (to the right) in the Timeline. This will place the newly selected clips before any footage that came after the insertion point.

CONNECT EDIT

Creating a connected clip by dragging is more useful and easier than performing either an Insert or Append edit by dragging. A Connect edit is useful when you want to add supporting footage (often called b-roll) to a scene.

Here's how the Connect edit command works.

1. Make sure your project has at least one clip added.

   Normally, this would be a sound bite or primary source of narration that serves as the basis for your primary storyline area in the Timeline and is used to build your initial sequence.

LOCATION IS EVERYTHING

Depending on where you drag the clips in the Timeline, your actions may result in an Append, an Insert, a Connect, or a Replace edit. Final Cut Pro automatically adjusts surrounding clips to fit in place around any clips that you've dragged.

NOT YOUR FATHER'S EDIT

Connect edits are slightly different than the other edit types in that they never add clips to the primary storyline. If you perform a Connect edit in an empty Timeline, Final Cut Pro first adds a gap clip to the primary storyline and attaches the new connected clip to it. (Think of a gap clip as a placeholder.)

2. Select one or more clips (or a range) in the Event Browser.

3. Specify where you want the clip to be connected in the Timeline.

   > Position the playhead over the insertion point in the primary storyline. This will then start the connected clip at that point.

   > Make a range selection in the primary story-line to limit the duration of the connected clip.

4. Click the Connect button in the toolbar (or press Q) to connect the selected clip(s) to the specified point in the Timeline. If you don't have a range selected, the insertion point will serve as the starting point for the connected clip. If you press Shift+Q, the insertion point will serve as an ending point for the connected clips.

   You can alternatively just drag your selection to the gray area above or below the primary story-line; the first frame of the source selection is connected to the primary storyline at the point where you released the mouse button.

It is important to remember that if you rearrange, move, ripple, or remove clips in the primary storyline, any clips connected to them will move (or be deleted) along with the primary storyline clips.

Gap Clips

As you edit, you'll sometimes need to hold a space in the Timeline for a clip that you don't have yet. Final Cut Pro X allows you to easily create a blank and silent clip called a *gap clip* (another term you may hear is a *slug*) that can be adjusted to any duration.

Using a gap clip is simple.

1. Move the playhead to the point in the primary storyline where you want to insert the gap.

   You can set an In and Out point to define the range for the gap if you'd like.

2. Choose Edit > Insert Gap (Option+W).

   Final Cut Pro X inserts a blank clip (containing blank video and silent audio) that you can adjust to any duration.

3. All clips after the insertion point are rippled forward (to the right).

If you didn't assign a duration, the gap clip by default is 3:00 long. Chances are you'll want to change this.

4. There are two ways to change the duration of the gap clip:

> Press Control+D to change the duration and enter your desired duration in minutes, seconds, and frames; for example, 20000 for 2 minutes or 1000 for ten seconds.

> Grab the right edge of the gap clip and drag it to the length you want.

To insert and configure a placeholder clip, position the playhead in the Timeline where you want to add the placeholder clip. Choose Edit > Insert Placeholder (Option+Command+W). Select the clip in the Timeline and press Command+4 to open it in the Inspector panel. The best way to see the variety of options available in this generator is simply to click through them.

TRY A PLACEHOLDER CLIP

If you don't yet have all the footage you need for your edit, you can insert an easy-to-configure storyboard style clip into your Timeline called a placeholder. A placeholder clip can provide a hint about what the final media will look like, such as the number of people, framing, and even location.

▲ The Placeholder clip is a useful way to identify missing footage while showing the composition and content of the clip to come.

Arranging Clips in the Timeline

After you have created your basic program, you may want or need to reorder some of your clips in the Timeline. For instance, you might want to start with a different concert shot that you used later in your story, or you might want to kick off with a sound bite that really grabs your viewer. More likely, your client or producer has said, "Hey can we move that shot earlier?" (or later—Final Cut Pro is pretty flexible).

With Final Cut Pro, you can do what comes intuitively. Click on the clip and drag it exactly where you need it. Because of the magnetic Timeline, everything snaps into place and any clips that are connected to the clip you are dragging will move right along with the primary clip.

Moving Clips By Dragging Horizontally

The most common type of movement for a clip is to reposition it left (or right) within the Timeline so it happens earlier (or later). These type of edits are common as you refine a story; you may know which clips you want to use, but rearranging their order can change the overall impact of the story.

To move clips by dragging, follow these steps.

1. Select one or more clips in your Timeline.

2. Drag the clips where you want them to go in the Timeline.

   You will see an outline of your selection (and dimmed video) at the new position in the Timeline.

Edit a Still Image with an External Image Editing Application

If you need to color correct or enhance a photo, it is often far faster to use a dedicated photo editing application. You can modify a still image with an external image editing application (such as Aperture or iPhoto), and the changes appear automatically in the clip in Final Cut Pro.

1. Select a still-image clip in your the Timeline.

2. Locate the clip's source media file in the Finder by Control-clicking the clip and choosing Reveal in Finder from the context menu (Command+Shift+R).

3. Open the source media file in the external image editing application.

4. In the image editing application, modify the image and save the changes.

5. Switch back to Final Cut Pro.

The changes to the source image should appear automatically in the still-image clip in Final Cut Pro. If not, you can drag in the new clip and replace the old in your Timeline.

3. Release your mouse button; the repositioned clip (or clips) are placed exactly where the outline was.

Don't panic if you misplace a clip when you drag. You can simply undo the move by choosing Edit > Undo (Command+Z).

Final Cut Pro will ripple any clips (and all the clips connected to those clips) in the Timeline to make room for the newly repositioned clips. It will also close the gap left by the clips that were moved.

Moving Clips By Dragging Vertically

Although dragging horizontally is more common, you may also need to drag clips vertically. In this case you are not changing when a clip occurs, but you may change how it is composited with other footage. The stacking order of a clip determines visibility. For example, you might scale a photo smaller and position it above a video track to create a split-screen composite.

If you pull a clip out of the primary storyline, it will become a connected clip, which you can drag to attach to any clip above it. You can also drag a clip below the primary storyline. This is usually used when mixing audio, but you can also move video below another video track. Why might you do this? If the clip on the main storyline has transparency, as in a chroma key or graphic, you can see through that transparent area to the clip under the primary storyline.

Here's how to move a clip vertically.

1. With the Select tool (A), select one or more clips.

These can come from the primary storyline or be used as connected clips.

A BETTER DRAG

If you need to be more precise when dragging, you can zoom into your Timeline by pressing Command+=. The increased magnification gives you greater accuracy. You can even use this keyboard shortcut after you have started dragging your clip.

2. Do one of the following:

> Drag the clips from the primary storyline to their new position as connected clips (above or below the primary storyline). By default, whenever you drag a clip out of the primary storyline, Final Cut Pro will always close the empty space left by the moved clip. This will affect the total duration of your project.

> You can also move connected clips back into the primary storyline: Drag the clips from their position as connected clips to an edit point between two clips in the primary storyline. The Timeline reacts exactly as if you did an Insert edit from the Event Browser. The "former connected clips" are inserted in the primary storyline, and the clips to the right of the edit point move farther right to make room for the new clips.

▲ Dragging a clip up makes it a connected clip (and will affect the duration of your storyline).

WHY CAN'T I ATTACH THIS CLIP?

If a clip already has a connected clip attached to it, you cannot drag it to the primary storyline and attach it to a third clip. All that will happen is a regular drag edit, with clips moving out of the way on the primary storyline. If there is a connected clip attached to the clip you need to move, you must either remove or attach the connected clip to another clip in the Timeline, or right-click the clip and choose Lift from Primary Storyline (Option+Command+up arrow).

Moving Clips By Entering a Timecode Value

There are lots of ways to rearrange your clips other than dragging. They are usually more precise and are used as you fine-tune your edit. You can use numerical editing, which is a fancy way of saying that you can type in a number to move clips left or right in your Timeline. Moving a clip left means it will happen earlier in the show and right means it will happen later.

To move a clip or group of clips in the Timeline numerically, follow these steps.

1. Select one or more clips in the Timeline.

2. You can move the selected items using keyboard shortcuts:

   › To move the clips forward, press the equals (=) key (think of it as the + key). Enter how far you want the clip to move. Remember that you are working in timecode, which means you need to enter 00 after minutes and seconds to represent frames. If all you type in is 10, you will move your clips by 10 frames, not 10 seconds (10 seconds is 1000). (You do not need to type in any colons or semicolons.)

   › To move the clips backward, press the minus (-) key, and enter an amount using the appropriate timecode format.

3. Press Return to apply the change.

When moving clips numerically in your Timeline, it is likely that you will overwrite some media; however, moving these clips back to the right will not return your Timeline to its original state. A gap clip will remain in place of the clips that were overwritten. You can choose Edit > Undo to get back the missing footage (but this will undo the edit).

Nudging Clips with Keyboard Shortcuts

The nudging feature in Final Cut Pro allows you to use your keyboard to move selected items by very small amounts, such as frames. It may not seem critical, but moving a clip a few frames forward or backward can sometime make or break how a scene feels.

To nudge one or more selected clips in the Timeline:

› Press comma (,) to nudge the clips left by one frame.

› Press Shift+comma (,) to move the selection left by 10 frames.

› Press period (.) to move the selection right by one frame.

Move Clips from and to the Primary Storyline Without Rippling the Project

You can move clips from and to the primary storyline without affecting the total duration of your project. This is useful if you've already locked down the duration of a scene or taken the time to precisely edit to music.

1. Select the clips you want to move.

2. To move selected clips from the primary storyline to connected clips at the same Timeline position, choose Edit > Lift from Primary Storyline (or press Command+Option+up arrow). Gap clips fill in the vacant parts of the primary storyline as needed.

3. To move selected connected clips to the primary storyline, choose Edit > Overwrite to Primary Storyline (or press Command+Option+down arrow).

Note that the Overwrite to Primary Storyline command is not available for audio-only clips.

> Press Shift+period (.) to move the selection right by 10 frames.

As with numerical entry, moved clips will overwrite any clips at the new location, and a gap clip will replace the empty space left in the Timeline.

You can also use similar shortcuts to precisely move audio in smaller distances:

> Press Option+comma (,) to move the selection left by one subframe.

> Press Shift+Option+comma (,) to move the selection left by 10 subframes.

> Press Option+period (.) to move the selection right by one subframe.

> Press Shift+Option+period (.) to move the selection right by 10 subframes.

Overwriting Clips with the Position Tool

Sometimes you'll just want to grab a clip and move it to a new location. You don't want to swap positions like you would with the dragging method, and you don't want to do any "numerical" math. You just want a clip to go "over there."

Well, if you just drag it to the right, it snaps right back to the end of the storyline. If you drag it to the left,

you always get some sort of Insert edit. This dragging back and forth with no results can be a little maddening. The key is to switch from the Select tool to the Position tool. This lets you move clips precisely without causing other clips to move to make room.

Here's how to perform an overwrite edit.

1. Choose the Position tool from the Tools menu in the toolbar or press P.

   The Select tool changes to the Position tool, which looks like an arrow without a tail.

2. Select the clip(s) you want to move.

3. Drag the clip(s) to a new position in the Timeline.

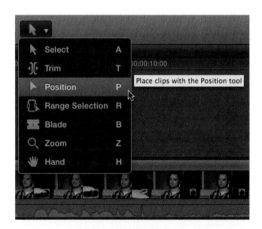

Pitfalls of Moving Clips with Numerical Entry and Keyboard Nudging

Moving clips around your Timeline by using numerical entry or nudging with a keyboard shortcut works very differently in Final Cut Pro than just dragging them. When you reposition a clip using these methods, you can actually overwrite part or all of the clips before or after the media you are moving. Final Cut Pro replaces the empty area that is left behind with a gap clip.

Although this can be annoying, it is not destructive. The original media is still available, and you can either undo to return the Timeline to its original state or perform a ripple edit on the truncated clip and add back the media. If you overwrite multiple clips, you will need to reedit them back into your Timeline.

Table 7.1 Shortcuts for Navigating the Timeline

TASK	KEYBOARD SHORTCUT
Fit the Timeline to the window	Choose View > Zoom to Fit (Shift+Z)
Zoom in to the Timeline	Command+equals (=)
Zoom out of the Timeline	Command+minus (-)

4. The moved clip(s) overwrite(s) any clips at the new position.

   A gap clip fills in the vacant part of the Timeline to prevent any rippling.

5. When you are done positioning clips, remember to switch back to the Select tool for standard editing.

Navigating the Timeline

By this point, you've probably figured out some of the ways to move around in the Timeline. Being able to quickly get to any point in your Timeline is critical to efficient editing. Final Cut Pro X gives you that power through a series of keyboard shortcuts and buttons that speed up your workflow.

Zooming and Scrolling in the Timeline

Depending on the duration of your show, you may need to do a lot of horizontal navigation in the Timeline.

Perhaps it's to zoom in to precisely control an edit point or to scroll through a long Timeline for an in-depth story.

Table 7.1 lists a few useful shortcuts for Timeline zooming and scrolling.

You can also zoom in to and out of the Timeline using the Zoom tool.

1. Select the Zoom tool by pressing Z.

2. To zoom in to the Timeline, click the section of the Timeline you want to zoom in to.

3. To zoom out of the Timeline, Option-click the section of the Timeline you want to zoom out of.

You can also scroll horizontally through a Timeline (if you are zoomed all the way out, this isn't necessary and won't work):

> Drag the slider at the bottom of the Timeline to the left or the right.

> Press H to switch to the Hand tool and drag left or right in the Timeline. (You can switch to the Hand tool temporarily by holding down the H key before you drag.)

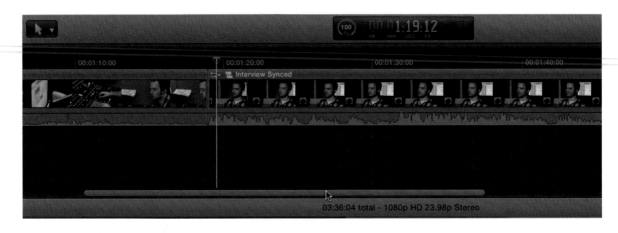

Adjusting Timeline Settings

Everybody is different; each editor prefers the Timeline to look a specific way. Sometimes you'll want to view tall filmstrip images; other times you'll want to see them smaller. Sometimes you'll want to see huge audio waveforms, and other times you won't want to see them at all.

Final Cut Pro provides the flexibility to view the Timeline in a variety of ways that matches the way you are editing at that moment. There are several adjustments you can make to how you view your clips. The two that you will use most are clip appearance and clip height.

To adjust clip appearance and height, follow these steps.

1. Click the Clip Appearance button in the lower-right corner of the Timeline.

2. Click one of the six Clip Appearance buttons at the top.

   There are six basic ways you can view the clips in your Timeline:

   > Audio waveforms only

   > Three variations of the size of the thumbnail in relation to the height of the waveforms

   > Thumbnails only

   > Clip name only

3. Drag the Clip Height slider to the left to decrease the clip height or to the right to increase the clip height.

Quick Navigation Techniques

Moving through your Timeline often requires precision (especially as you start to refine a program). Fortunately, Final Cut Pro X offers many precision controls.

Navigate frame by frame:

> To move backward in one-frame increments, press the left arrow key.

> To move forward in one-frame increments, press the right arrow key.

> To move in ten-frame increments, hold the Shift modifier key while pressing either arrow key.

Navigate between edit points:

> To jump between edit points, use the up and down arrow keys:

> Press the up arrow key to move to the previous edit.

> Press the down arrow key to move to the following (next) edit.

Snapping

You may notice that when you move your playhead over an edit point, it clings to the edge of the clip. When you drag a connected clip along the main storyline, it too wants to stick to each edit point. This is called *snapping*. It is a great Final Cut Pro feature because usually you want all your clips to line up perfectly with each other.

Other times you may want to move a clip just a few frames but can't. The reason is that the snapping feature has become a liability, grabbing the clip and pulling it in like a black hole. Fortunately, you can easily turn snapping on and off, even while you're dragging

a clip. Press the N key to toggle snapping on and off or click the Snapping button in the upper-right corner of the Timeline. When snapping is on, the Snapping button appears blue.

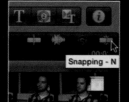

Navigate to the beginning or the end of your program:

> If you want to jump to the beginning of your program, press the Home key.

> Press the End key to jump to the last frame of your program.

> If you're working on a laptop or a keyboard without a Home or End key, press the function key (fn) and the left and right arrow keys to quickly jump to the beginning and end of your Timeline.

Navigate by entering time:

To jump to a specific point in time on your Timeline, click once in the center of the Dashboard (or press Control+P), enter the time value of where you want to go, and press Return. For example, if you want to move the playhead to exactly two minutes in, press Control+P, enter 20000, and press Return.

Navigating Using the Timeline Index

The Timeline Index is located in the lower-left corner of the Final Cut Pro window. When you first launch the application, it is hidden. To reveal it, click the Timeline Index button in the lower-left corner of the Final Cut Pro main window (or press Command+Shift+2). You can hide it with the same command or button click.

The Timeline Index provides a text-based view of the clips in the Timeline, which is a fancy way of looking at your edit in list form. You can easily filter the Timeline Index to show only the items you want to see. You can filter by clip type, such as Video, Audio, and Titles, and you can filter by clip name.

You can also use the Timeline Index to navigate through the Timeline. When you click on a clip in the index, the

Working with Still Images

As a photographer, it's natural for you to use still images in the creation of your project. You can add still images to your project from the Event Browser or the Photos Browser.

THE EVENT BROWSER

Adding a still image from the Event Browser is easy. Just import the still image into an event, and then select the still image like you would a clip. After a still image is imported, it functions like any other clip in Final Cut Pro. You can use any of the techniques described in this chapter to add still-image clips to the Timeline.

THE PHOTOS BROWSER

Another convenient way to access images (especially if you're using Aperture or iPhoto) is the Photos Browser. To add a still image from the Photos Browser, follow these steps.

1. Open the Photos Browser. You can sort by application as well as view events or albums.

2. Select a still image or images.

3. Drag the selected item(s) directly into the Timeline.

DURATION OF PHOTOS

The default duration for still images is four seconds, but you can change this default setting in the Editing pane of Final Cut Pro preferences.

There is no limit on the duration of a still-image clip. To adjust the duration of a still-image clip in the Timeline, use any of the trimming techniques described in this chapter. To adjust the duration of multiple still-image clips at once, select the clips and choose Modify > Change Duration (Control+D).

playhead will jump to the point in the Timeline where that clip is used. Conversely, when you play a project, you will see a small horizontal playhead moving down the list of items in the Timeline Index.

Here are some useful functions of the Timeline Index:

> You can rename clips directly in the Timeline Index.

> You can add or review notes in the Notes column. To edit, simply double-click in the area you want to modify and start typing.

> You can specify which columns are displayed by Control-clicking a column heading and choosing an option from the context menu.

> The Timeline Index can also help you sort through other parameters, such as markers, to-do items, roles, keywords, and much more.

> The most useful role the Timeline Index plays for us is that it's a great way to keep track of where a clip was used in the Timeline and jump to that clip quickly (by clicking on its name).

▲ The Timeline Index is a quick way to see a list of all clips in your Timeline.

CHAPTER 8

Advanced Editing

By now you should be halfway to completing your project. You've framed out your basic story using the primary storyline as well as added b-roll and connected shots. Now it's time to take your edit to the next level by precisely refining its rhythm. You'll want to swap out some lesser shots with better takes. You'll also need to work on pacing and rhythm by modifying what happens when. This is what advanced editing is all about.

Advanced Editing Commands

It's time to expand your editing skills beyond Append edits, Insert edits, and Connect edits. There are two more types of edits that that can help you fine-tune a show: the Overwrite edit and the Replace edit. At first blush, they both sound pretty similar, and they are. But there is one distinct difference—timing.

Overwrite Edit

The Overwrite edit is a precise edit based on time. You can set the time in the Event Browser by selecting a clip's range (with In and Out points) or in the Timeline (with In and Out points). Unlike an Insert edit or Append edit, an Overwrite edit will not make your show any longer. The new media deletes the selected range in your Timeline and replaces it with new media. The key word here is range, because you can overwrite part of a clip or several clips. At first, it may be difficult to understand how Final Cut Pro "thinks" when performing an Overwrite edit, so remember your Undo and Redo commands.

Overwrite edits are great for several uses:

> If you need to cover a sound bite that has a fixed duration.

> If you're cutting to the beat with a music track.

> Anytime that the duration of the shot in your Timeline is more important than the duration of the action in the event media.

> You can also back-time a shot so that the edit ends at the same time the action is finished.

WHAT'S MY POINT?
By default, the Overwrite edit will use the selected range. If no range is selected, the start point will be at the playhead or skimmer position. If you've edited with other nonlinear editing systems, an Overwrite edit in Final Cut Pro X could also be thought of as a three-point edit.

Here's how to overwrite clips in the Timeline with clips from the Event Browser:

1. Select one or more clips in the Event Browser.

2. Define where you want the overwrite clip to start in the Timeline:

   > Position the playhead where you want the Overwrite edit to go.

   > Select a range within one clip or across multiple clips in the Timeline.

3. Choose Edit > Overwrite (D).

The source clip appears in the primary storyline and overwrites any clips for the duration set in the source clip. Yes; reread that previous sentence. The duration of the edit is based solely on the duration of the selection or selections in your Event Browser. Final Cut Pro uses only the "In" part of the range for its reference point. If you need to perform a back-time edit using the overwrite clip's Out point, press Shift+D.

CONTROLLING THE ORDER OF CLIPS

If there are multiple source clips in the selection, the clips will appear in the Timeline in the order in which they were selected. Hold down the Command key as you select clips to set the order you want them to be in the Timeline.

A COUPLE OF OVERWRITE GOTCHAS

The Overwrite command ignores whole clip selections in the Timeline. If you don't select a range in the Timeline, Final Cut Pro positions the start of the overwrite clip at the playhead or skimmer position. Also, if you use the keyboard shortcut and the skimmer is present in the Timeline, the edit will occur at the skimmer position.

Replace Edit

The basic Replace edit simply swaps out one clip for another. You can grab the new media from the Event Browser, Final Cut Pro's media browsers, or the Finder. If the new clip is shorter, your Timeline will ripple to the left and your show gets shorter. If the clip is longer, your entire Timeline ripples to the right, lengthening your program.

Now, you might be asking yourself, why would I want that to happen? Simple; suppose you have two different reads of a performance. One takes 16 seconds, and the other is better but longer at 20 seconds. You don't want to have to move all your other clips to the right just to fit in that extra 4 seconds. Final Cut Pro will do it for you.

Replace edits are a great way of swapping out one shot for another. Keep in mind that in contrast to Overwrite edits, a Replace edit does not work on a range of a clip or multiple clips. It is a one-for-one, all-or-nothing option. It works on *whole* Timeline clips only, and if the new clip is a different length than the clip it is replacing, it could change the duration of your project. Depending on the type of project you are editing, the entirety of the scene is more important than the precise duration of a replaced shot.

With that said, the Replace clip function is extremely robust. In addition to the standard Replace, you can replace using the start or end of the source clip. The duration is matched to the clip in the Timeline; you decide whether the end or beginning of the media gets trimmed. You can also create an audition or add to an audition.

Here's how to replace a clip in the Timeline with one or more clips:

1. Select a clip or range of a clip in the Event Browser.

2. Drag the source selection over the clip in the Timeline you want to replace.

3. A white highlight will surround the clip in the Timeline.

4. When you release the mouse button, a menu will appear.

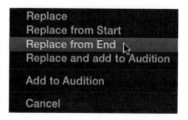

▲ The shortcut menu shows your options for the Replace edit.

5. Choose *one* of the options:

 › **Replace.** The Timeline clip is replaced with the new clip. If the source clip is longer or shorter, the Timeline will ripple to accommodate the duration change.

 › **Replace from Start.** The Timeline clip is replaced with the source clip, starting from the *beginning* of the source selection. The length of the Timeline clip determines the duration.

REPLACE EDIT KEYBOARD SHORTCUTS
With a clip selected in both the Event Browser and the Timeline, use these shortcuts:

 › Replace edit (Shift+R)
 › Replace from Start edit (Option+R)
 › Replace and add to Audition (Shift+Y)

WARNING OR BENEFIT— YOU MAKE THE CALL
If the range or source clip you select in the browser is shorter than that of the Timeline clip and there are available handles (the extra media beyond your selected In or Out point), Final Cut Pro will extend the duration of your source clip to match the target clip's duration.

 › **Replace from End.** The Timeline clip is replaced with the source clip, starting from the *end* of the source selection. The length of the Timeline clip determines the duration.

 › **Replace and add to Audition.** The Timeline clip is replaced, and an audition is created. The original clip is held as an alternate. If the source clip is longer or shorter, the Timeline will ripple to accommodate the duration change.

 › **Add to Audition.** The Timeline clip does not appear to change. However, it does become added to an audition. The new clip is attached as an alternate pick inside the audition. Because nothing was really switched, the audition clip's length stays the same. When you cycle through the alternate clips in the audition, the clip's length and Timeline's duration may change.

 › **Cancel.** The Replace edit is canceled.

6. The source clip appears in the Timeline (unless you chose Add to Audition or Cancel).

Auditions

Final Cut Pro allows you to easily group related clips into sets, called *auditions*, from which you can choose one clip to use. You can create an audition composed of different clips to try out multiple takes, or you can create an audition composed of multiple versions of the same clip to preview different effects. Auditions appear in the Event Browser and Timeline as clips with an Audition icon in the upper-left corner.

The audition's filmstrip displays the currently selected clip, called the *pick*. All other clips in the audition are referred to as *alternates*. You can open an audition to see the selected clip and the alternates.

Auditions allow you to preserve your alternate edits without affecting the other clips in the Timeline. When you're not auditioning the clips in an audition, the audition functions like an individual clip. You can trim an audition, apply transitions between auditions and other clips, and add keywords and markers. You can keep your audition containing your alternate clips for as long as necessary.

Adding Only a Clip's Video or Audio

There will be times when you'll want to use just the video or audio from a clip in your Timeline. For example, perhaps the cut-away (or b-roll) you want to connect to your Timeline has distracting audio, or you recorded a voice-over track and the video is just an image of the inside of the lens cap. Instead of bringing in both the audio and video and then deleting the unnecessary track, Final Cut Pro allows you to isolate just the media you want to bring in.

Here's how to make video-only or audio-only edits.

1. Click the Edit pop-up menu in the toolbar.

> To edit in just video, choose Video Only from the Edit menu in the toolbar (or press Option+2).

> To edit just the audio, choose Audio Only from the Edit menu in the toolbar (or press Option+3).

2. The edit buttons in the toolbar change their appearance to indicate the mode you selected.

3. Add clips to the Timeline as you normally would.

4. To return to the default (video and audio) mode, choose All from the Edit menu in the toolbar (or press Option+1).

The gotcha here is being your own worst enemy and not switching back to the default setting where both the video and audio of a clip come in simultaneously. Getting used to using the keyboard shortcuts to toggle between the default settings, video only, and audio only will prevent a lot of editing headaches.

Removing a Clip

Nobody's perfect; there will be times when you'll want (or even need) to remove a clip, group of clips, or even part of a clip from your Timeline. The reality is that removing a clip is very simple and can be quite precise as long as you take into account a few key strategies.

Remember that Final Cut Pro by its nature is nondestructive. So when you delete a clip from the Timeline, it will still remain in your Event Library (and on your hard drive). If you delete a clip from an Event by mistake, you can always bring it back with an Undo (Command+Z) or a reimport.

DELETE CLIPS OR RANGES FROM THE TIMELINE

1. Select the clips in the Timeline or the range from a single clip you want to remove.

2. Choose Edit > Delete (or press the Delete key).

   The clips or portions of clips are removed from the Timeline, and any clips to the right of the selection ripple to close the gap.

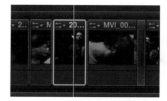 

DELETE CLIPS OR RANGES WITHOUT AFFECTING THE TOTAL PROJECT DURATION AND TIMING

If you want to remove clips from the Timeline but still maintain the total project duration and timing, you can replace clips with gap clips. This method prevents any Ripple edits.

1. Select the clips or range you want to remove.

2. Choose Edit > Replace with Gap (or press Shift+Delete).

Final Cut Pro replaces the selection in the Timeline with a gap clip.

Isolating Clips During Editing

When editing, you'll sometimes want to focus on a single clip. Isolating a clip is great if you want to focus on the main interview and not see all the b-roll and graphics you placed above it. This process is called *soloing*, and it essentially features one or more items by themselves so you can make a discerning decision.

For audio, here's how to solo one or more selected items.

1. In the Timeline, select one or multiple audio clips you want to isolate.

2. Choose Clip > Solo (Option+S). You can also click the Solo button in the upper-right corner of the Timeline.

When solo is turned on, the Solo button turns yellow, and non-soloed clips are shown in black and white.

3. To turn off solo, click the Solo button again (Option+S).

You can also disable a whole group of clips so they don't distract you during the creative process. When you disable a clip and then play back or output your Timeline, the disabled clips are not part of the program. This works well if you're trying out different b-roll footage or different sound tracks. The great thing about disabling a clip (instead of deleting) is the ability to bring the clip back into use. All you need to do is reenable it.

Here's how to disable one or more clips.

1. Select one or more clips in the Timeline.

2. Choose Clip > Disable (V).

A great way to remember this shortcut is to think V for Visible.

 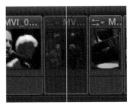

Disabled clips are dimmed in the Timeline and are invisible and silent during playback.

3. To reenable the disabled clips, select them in the Timeline and choose Clip > Disable (or press V).

What Happens to Connected Clips?

There are two ways that connected clips are handled when you delete an item from the Timeline:

> **Delete Only.** If you select an entire Timeline clip (for example, with the C key) or a range over an entire clip (for example, with the X key) and delete it, any connected clips or storylines are also deleted. If you select a partial range of a clip that includes a connected clip or storyline, the connected clip will not be deleted. Instead, the connected items are shifted to the closest primary storyline clip.

> **Replace with Gap.** This method preserves connected clips. When you replace a clip with a gap clip, any connected clips will be attached to the resulting gap clip.

Trimming Your Edits

Trimming is useful to fine-tune the timing of your edits. Editing is all about fractions of a second. A cut a second (or even frames) too early or too late can affect how your viewer perceives a sequence. As an editor, you often need to watch how your shots flow in the Timeline.

Sometimes this fine-tuning involves changing the moment a cut happens; sometimes it is determining whether a shot needs to just end sooner or last longer. Other times, a shot might be perfect, like a reaction shot, but it happens too soon or too late in the sequence of events. In Final Cut Pro, you can use a variety of techniques, such as Ripple edits, Roll edits, Slip edits, and Slide edits, to trim Timeline clips and edit points.

Find a Timeline Clip's Source

When editing, you often need to find the original location of the clip you are using in the Timeline, whether from the Event Browser or even at the Finder level of your hard drive. If you've only used a handful of clips and have only a dozen or so clips in your Event Browser, this is easy. But imagine having several thousand clips in your Event Browser and hundreds of clips in your Timeline.

Final Cut Pro allows you to easily find these source clips with a click of the mouse or a keystroke. When you find the original clip, you can look at its neighbors for the alternative shot you want.

FIND AND REVEAL THE SOURCE EVENT CLIP FOR A TIMELINE CLIP

1. In the Timeline, select the clip whose source Event clip you want to locate.

If the Event Browser is in Filmstrip view, a selection border appears around the source clip in the Event Browser, and the playhead position in the source clip matches the playhead position in the Timeline clip.

FIND AND REVEAL THE FINDER LOCATION FOR A TIMELINE CLIP

You may also want to find where an original clip is located on a hard drive.

1. In the Timeline or an Event, select the clip whose source you want to locate.

2. Choose Clip > Reveal in Finder (or press Command+Shift+R). If you chose not to "Copy files to Final Cut Events folder," this will reveal the media file's alias. In the Finder, choose File > Show Original to reveal the original media.

The Ripple Edit: Extend or Shorten a Clip

If all you want to do is extend the length of a clip and push everything else down the Timeline—for instance, to let a shot breathe a bit before cutting away from it—the Ripple Edit tool is the answer. It also lets you trim the end of a shot that may linger a bit too long, and it automatically closes the gap the removed media creates. Keep in mind that you can trim a clip in your project by adjusting either the start point or end point of the clip.

RIPPLE EDIT POINTS WITH THE SELECT TOOL

It's easy to adjust the timing of an edit using the standard Select tool. Here's how.

1. In the Timeline, position your pointer at the start or the end of the clip you want to trim.

Notice that the pointer automatically changes from an arrow icon to a trim icon.

SAFE TO TRIM

No matter how you trim or make other edits in Final Cut Pro, the original media is never modified. Trimmed or deleted pieces of clips are removed from your project only, not from the clips in your Event Library or from the media files on your hard drive.

JUST KEEP WORKING

To perform a Ripple edit, you don't need to change from the default Select tool (A). With the paradigm of connected clips, you no longer need to worry about items in your Timeline getting out of sync.

2. Examine whether the tool (a small filmstrip) points to the left or to the right. If it points to the left, you will affect the outbound or first clips of the pair. If it points to the right, you will affect the incoming or second clip of the pair.

3. Drag the start point or the end point in the direction you want to trim the clip.

As you drag, the clip shortens or lengthens. A numerical value (in frames and seconds) indicates the amount of time you are moving the edit point. Any clips to the right of the edit point will be rippled accordingly.

PERFORMING A RIPPLE EDIT WITH THE KEYBOARD

If you don't want to drag and edit to perform a Ripple edit, like many other actions in Final Cut Pro you can use numerical entry or keyboard shortcuts.

1. Select the side of the clip you want to perform the Ripple edit on. The yellow highlight will indicate which side you will affect.

2. Use *one* of these keyboard methods to control the Ripple edit:

   › Press the plus (+) key or the minus (–) key followed by the timecode duration to add or subtract from the current edit, and then press Return.

> Position the playhead or skimmer at a point in the Timeline to which you want to move the edit point, and press Shift+X (or choose Edit > Extend Edit).

If you extend a clip to its maximum length, meaning you used all the clip's available media, the clip edge will change from yellow to red.

▲ As you type a number, the duration updates to show you the impending change.

The Roll Edit: Change the Timing Between Two Clips

There are times when the combined duration of two adjacent clips is perfect. For example, let's say you are filling a ten-second space and you've placed two shots that are five seconds long sequentially in the Timeline. However, the rhythm of the piece dictates that the timing of the cut point needs to be changed. So shot one would be better suited to be three seconds long, and shot two should be seven seconds long. The best solution here is to perform a Roll edit.

SWITCH TO TRIMMING TEMPORARILY
To switch to the Trim tool temporarily, hold down the T key. When you release the T key, the tool reverts to the previously active tool.

A Roll edit simply adds media to one clip in the pair as you remove it from the other clip in the pair. The duration of your Timeline never changes, but the rhythm of the edit can change dramatically.

ROLL EDIT POINTS WITH THE TRIM TOOL

Because rolling is not the primary method for editing in Final Cut Pro X, you'll need to change from the Select tool (A) to the Trim tool (T).

1. Choose the Trim tool from the Tools menu in the toolbar (or press T).

2. In the Timeline, click the edit point you want to roll. (You will see that both sides of the edit point are selected.)

3. Drag the edit point left or right.

Nudging Edit Points with the Keyboard

If you only need to adjust an edit point by a frame or two, nudging is the perfect solution. Nudging works for both Ripple and Roll edits the same way. You can move the edit point by one or more video frames.

1. Select the start or end point of the clip you want to trim. Use the Select tool to Ripple or the Trim tool to Roll.

2. To move the edit point, do any of the following:

   > To move the edit point left by one frame, press Comma (,).

   > To move the edit point left by ten frames, press Shift+Comma (,).

   > To move the edit point right by one frame, press Period (.).

PERFORMING A ROLL EDIT WITH THE KEYBOARD

If you don't want to drag and edit to perform a Roll edit, you can use numerical entry or keyboard shortcuts for precise control.

1. Select the edit between the clips you want to perform the Roll edit on.

2. Use the *one* of these keyboard methods to control the Roll edit:

   › Press the plus (+) key or the minus (–) key followed by the timecode duration to add or subtract from the current edit, and then press Return.

   › Position the playhead or skimmer at a point in the Timeline to which you want to move the edit point, and press Shift+X (or choose Edit > Extend Edit).

The edit point is rolled to the new location. The combined duration of the two clips stays the same.

Trim the Start or End of a Clip at the Playhead

There are times when all you'll want to do is trim off the beginning or the end of a clip and not go through all the trouble of selecting and dragging. Perhaps you want to trim off an "um" at the beginning of an interview or cut before a mistake happens in the shot. You can easily trim off these ranges with a single command, even while playing back the project.

1. Select the clip that you want to trim.

2. In the Timeline, position the playhead or the skimmer on the frame at which you want to trim the clip.

Show Detailed Trimming Feedback

We recommend selecting "Show detailed trimming feedback" in Final Cut Pro preferences. This display is available for Ripple, Roll, Slip, and Slide edits, as well as for trimming in the Precision Editor. For example, when performing a Roll edit, you will see a "two-up" display in the Viewer that shows the end point of the left clip and the start point of the right clip. Note that when dragging, the frame being trimmed is displayed in the Viewer. If this preference is not enabled, hold down the Option key during the drag to display the opposite frame.

To turn on detailed trimming feedback, follow these steps.

1. Choose Final Cut Pro > Preferences.

2. Click Editing.

3. In the Timeline section, select the "Show detailed trimming feedback" check box. The "two-up" display appears in the Viewer whenever you use a supported edit type or when trimming in the Precision Editor.

▲ The "Show detailed trimming feedback" option gives you better trimming feedback in the Viewer. If you don't see this view when trimming, choose Final Cut Pro > Preferences and select the detailed trimming option.

3. Use *one* of the following methods to trim:

> ❯ To trim off the start of the clip, choose Edit > Trim Start (Option+[).

> ❯ To trim off the end of the clip, choose Edit > Trim End (Option+]).

The clip is trimmed to the playhead (or skimmer) position, and the Timeline updates accordingly. In the case of connected clips or storylines, Final Cut Pro trims the selected clip. If there is no selection, Final Cut Pro trims the topmost clip.

The Slip Edit: Adjusting In and Out Points Simultaneously

Sometimes a clip occurs at the right time in your Timeline but shows the wrong media. A Slip edit allows you to change a clip's start and end points simultaneously. It doesn't change a clip's position or duration in the Timeline, but instead changes what portion of the clip's media the viewer sees (think slipping in place).

So why might you want to perform a Slip edit? Suppose you've cut your show perfectly, but upon later review you realize that in the group-wide shot is a guy glancing into the camera just before it cut away. All you want to do is roll the entire clip a few seconds so that his glance occurs beyond the edit point. Another example might be a music video where each cut needs to be right on the beat of the music. A Slip edit allows you to reposition what happens between the In and Out points without changing the timing and rhythm of your piece. Surrounding clips are not affected, and the overall duration of your project doesn't change.

Before you use a Slip edit for the first time, make sure the option "Show detailed trimming feedback" is selected in the Final Cut Pro preferences. When you perform a Slip edit, the "two-up" display shows the new start and end points of the clip you're slipping.

Here's how to perform a Slip edit.

1. Choose the Trim tool from the Tools menu in the toolbar (or press T).

The pointer changes to the Trim tool icon.

2. Click on the clip you need to modify, and then drag it left or right.

As you drag, a time numerical pop-up will indicate how much you're moving the start point and the end point. Yellow edge selections on the start point and end point indicate a Slip edit. If either the start point or the end point turns red as you drag, you've reached the end of the available media for that side of the clip.

3. When you are happy with the new In and Out points, release your mouse.

WHY CAN'T I SLIP?
To perform a Slip edit, you must have enough media on either side of the clip. We referred to this earlier as media handles. If you're having trouble slipping a clip, check that the clip has media handles on both sides. The Precision Editor is a perfect tool for this.

SLIP WITH THE KEYBOARD
Once a clip is selected with the Trim tool, you can also type in either a positive value + 0000 or a negative value – 0000 to slip the clip's In and Out points.

You can also perform a Slip edit using the keyboard. This lets you nudge edit points in the Timeline using any of the following shortcuts:

> To nudge the edit points left by one frame, press Comma (,).

> To nudge the edit points left by ten frames, press Shift+Comma (,).

> To nudge the edit points right by one frame, press Period (.).

> To nudge the edit points right by ten frames, press Shift+Period (.).

The Slide Edit: Moving a Clip in the Timeline

A Slide edit is similar to a Slip edit. Let's say that you are in the same situation where the length of the edit is perfect except this time it happens a bit too early or too late in your Timeline for aesthetic reasons. Maybe you cut to a performance shot during an interview, but it feels a little too early. If so, you can move the entire shot later in the storyline. Or maybe you cut to the identity of the killer but want to build a bit more suspense. You could simply slide the cut-away a second or two later, which could make all the difference.

SLIDE WITH THE KEYBOARD
You can perform a Slide edit using the same keyboard shortcuts as a Slip edit. Just make sure that you Option+select the edit in the Timeline with the Trim tool before pressing the keyboard shortcuts.

The Precision Editor

The Precision Editor provides an expanded view of the clips on either side of the edit point by showing you the unused media of each clip.

To activate the Precision Editor, double-click an edit point that you want to trim in the Timeline, or select an edit and press Control+E. You'll see two layers representing an expanded view of your outgoing and incoming clips.

The vertical line in the center of the Precision Editor is your cut point. The outgoing clip and the clips before it appear in the top part of the storyline. The incoming clip and the clips after it appear in the bottom part.

The clips that are to the right and left of the vertical edit line are dimmed; they represent the unused portions of media that are available. You can skim over these dimmed areas and play them back, which will help you decide where you might want to move your edit point:

> To perform a Roll edit, grab the small circular button in between the two rows of clips and drag left or right as needed.

> To perform a Ripple edit, click on either the upper

> Once you click, your cursor will change to a hand icon. You can then drag the end point of the outgoing clip or the start point of the incoming clip.

> You can perform a Ripple edit by skimming over the dimmed area of the outgoing clip or the incoming clip and then clicking on any point.

> To quickly navigate to another edit point, click the other edit point in the center line or use the up arrow or down arrow keys to jump to the next or previous edit point.

> To close the Precision Editor, double-click the current edit point or press the Esc key.

With a Slide edit, the clip's content and duration remain the same; only its position in the Timeline changes.

1. Choose the Trim tool from the Tools menu in the toolbar (T).

2. Option-click a clip to select it, and then drag it left or right. Yellow selections face out, indicating that you are performing a Slide edit.

Release the Option key while dragging to see the "two-up" display.

3. As you drag, a numeric value indicates the amount of time you're moving the clip in the Timeline.

The clips on either side of the clip that you are sliding must have enough media to fill in the empty area created by your move. (Again, we refer to this as handles.) When you run out of handles, your slide will simply stop, and you'll see a red highlight instead of a yellow highlight on the clip with no remaining media.

4. When you release the mouse button, the sliding clip stays in the new position in the Timeline.

5. The adjacent clips are trimmed to accommodate the change in the clip's position.

When you slide a clip, the adjacent clips get longer and shorter to accommodate the change in the clip's position. If you slide your clip to the left (so it's earlier in your show), clip one gets shorter and clip three (to the right of the sliding clip) gets longer. If you slide your clip to the right, so the cut-away comes later, the reverse happens. It's important to note that the combined duration of these three clips stays the same, and the project's total duration remains unchanged as well.

Working with Markers

Markers are simple reference points you can place on clips in your Timeline that you can use to locate, identify, and annotate specific frames. In editing, markers have several uses:

> You can use a marker to synchronize two or more clips at a specific point. For example, you might want to sync a specific sound effect with action on the screen or a sound bite with specific action in a b-roll shot.

> You can use markers (blue markers) to flag a specific location in a clip so you can easily find editing notes.

> You can also use markers to tag to-do items (red markers) and completed to-do items (green markers).

Add a Marker

One of the easiest ways to use markers is to identify elements in the Timeline. With just a few keystrokes or clicks, you can quickly add some organization.

1. Skim (or play) to the desired location, and stop playback when the playhead reaches the spot where you want to add a marker.

2. Choose Mark > Markers > Add Marker (M).

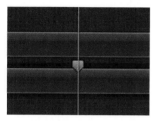

▲ A new marker is added to the primary story-line. Alternatively, you can select an attached clip before pressing the M key to add a marker on a specific clip.

If desired, you can create a marker and open the information box associated with the marker by choosing Mark > Markers > Add Marker and Modify (Option+M).

Remember that markers only live inside a clip, not on your Timeline. When you move a clip, all associated markers move with it. If you create a marker in a clip prior to bringing it into your Timeline, it will appear in the Timeline. Once a clip is edited into the Timeline, its markers become independent. Changes made to either the original clip or Timeline version will not affect one another.

MARKERS ALSO WORK IN THE EVENT BROWSER
If you added markers to clips in the Event Browser, they will be visible in both Filmstrip view and List view. When you add clips with markers to the Timeline, the markers are visible in both the Timeline and the Timeline Index.

MARK ON THE FLY
Just press the M key while playing the Timeline to add markers on the fly.

JUMP BETWEEN MARKERS
To jump between markers, you can use the keyboard. Press Control+Apostrophe (') to go to the next marker. Press Control+ Semicolon (;) to go to the previous marker.

DELETE DOESN'T DELETE MARKERS
As tempting as it may be, don't use the Delete key to delete a marker. Remember that in the Timeline pressing Delete will delete a clip; in the Event Browser pressing Delete will reject the frame with the marker.

Remove a Marker

Once you've resolved an issue or achieved sync, you might decide to remove markers. Although they don't affect your output, many treat markers or the information in them as a checklist of tasks to do for completing a sequence.

To remove a marker, do any of the following:

› Navigate to a marker and choose Mark > Markers > Delete Marker (Control+M).

› Select one or more clips, and then choose Mark > Markers > Delete Markers in Selection.

› Double-click a marker to open the Marker window, and then click the Delete button.

Modify Markers

As you work with markers, you'll often need to change them, perhaps to check off items on a to-do list or add additional notes about how a clip should be used. Markers are extremely flexible and aid in bringing organization to your workflow.

Here's how to view or modify a marker's information.

1. Double-click the desired marker.

   The Marker window opens above the marker.

2. You can then change the marker's information to suit your needs:

   > Enter descriptive text for the marker.

   > Click the Make To Do Item button to use the marker to track progress. The marker turns red for an incomplete task.

   > Once a to-do item is complete, you can select the Completed check box (the marker turns green to indicate a completed status).

3. When you're finished, click Done.

NUDGE A MARKER

You can adjust a marker's position right from the keyboard. To nudge a marker one frame to the right, press Control+Period (.). To nudge one frame to the left, press Control+Comma (,).

COPY AND PASTE MARKERS

If you want to reuse or move a marker, you can use word processor–like commands. Just right-click on a marker and choose Cut or Copy Marker. To add the marker back to a clip, just choose Edit > Paste to add the marker at the new location.

Adding Transitions

In video a *transition* is simply a way to get from point A (the end of one clip) to point B (the beginning of the next clip). If you've edited your program properly, a simple cut is most often the best choice to use for a transition.

During the concert segments of our program, we can use cuts between synced camera angles. To move from the concert into an interview segment, a dissolve is more appropriate. The use of an animated transition is often reserved to indicate a change in time or space (and softens the abruptness of a cut).

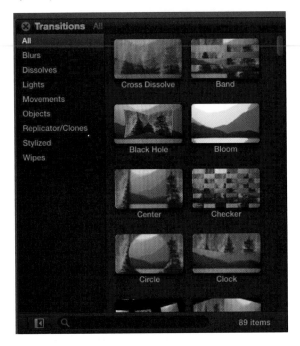

Although these two standards will work in most cases, there are a variety of transitions you can use in a program to solve problems. For example, a Bloom transition tightens up abrupt cuts in an interview when no b-roll footage is available. You can use a more dramatic animated wipe to transition between two distinct segments in a longer video. Audio transitions are equally important. Some of these include fade-in, fade-out, and crossfade (dissolve) to smooth rough audio edits. The best rule of thumb is *less is more*. Most of your transitions should be cuts and dissolves.

Transition Overlap and Handles

The trickiest aspect of transitions for new editors to wrap their head around is that transitions require overlapping media from the clips on each side of the edit. A one-second transition requires ½ second of video from the end of the left clip and ½ second of video from the start of the right clip. You don't need to have this video in the Timeline, but it must be part of the original clip. The trick is to always roll a bit early and let the camera roll after the take is finished.

Adding Standard Transitions

There are several methods you can use to add transitions to your project. Once a transition is added to your Timeline, you can adjust its parameters: its length, direction, how it interacts with the footage, and if you have Apple Motion Application, you can modify it even further.

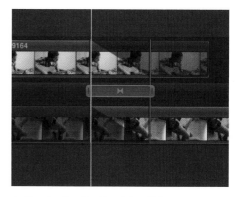

▲ By viewing the Precision Editor, you can better understand how the available handles on a clip impact transitions.

TRANSITIONS CAN DRAMATICALLY AFFECT THE PACING OF YOUR SHOW
A fast-paced show with long transitions is a recipe for disaster. Conversely, a slow-paced documentary can be equally ruined by an over-the-top transition. Always show restraint and match the style of transition to the program you're editing.

Critical Preference Settings for Transitions

Before placing transitions into your Timeline, double-check your Preference settings. Choose Final Cut Pro > Preferences (or press Command+Comma), and click the first icon for editing in the upper-left corner:

› **Default Duration.** The default of one second is fine, but we find that .5 seconds keep the show moving along at a good pace. (Don't worry; you can always change a transition's duration after you have placed it in the Timeline.)

› **Available Media (Recommended).** Final Cut Pro uses only the available handles on each side of the transition. The total duration of your project is unchanged. If one or both of the clips do not have enough extra media to support at least a four-frame transition, no transition is added. You will be given the option of using the Full Overlap mode for that transition.

› **Full Overlap.** The two clips are overlapped by the default length of the transition. Final Cut Pro will actually perform Ripple edits on each side of the transition to ensure that you have enough media for the full default duration of the transition. The total duration of your project decreases by whatever amount Final Cut Pro needs to Ripple edit your clips to make the transition work.

ADD A CROSS DISSOLVE

A standard cross dissolve can be used to fade between two clips. This is the most common effect you'll use in a project (after cut).

1. Click on the edit point of a clip in the Timeline with the Select tool.

   One or both clip edges should be highlighted. Don't worry; Final Cut Pro knows you want to put a transition across the clips. If you select a whole clip in the Timeline instead of just an edit point, transitions are added at each end of the selected clip.

2. Choose Edit > Add Cross Dissolve (Command+T).

3. Play back the clip to see the transition in real time.

ADD OR CHANGE A TRANSITION USING THE TRANSITIONS BROWSER

If you want to modify a transition, Final Cut Pro offers excellent controls in the Transitions Browser. Depending on which transition you've added, the controls will vary.

1. Click the Transitions button in the toolbar.

   It looks like a square with two triangles pointing toward each other. You will see a list of transitions and preview icons representing how each one looks. If you do not see the list, click the small Show/Hide button at the bottom of the Effects Browser.

2. Browse over 75 different types of transitions. You can refine the list by clicking on the type of transitions you want—blurs, dissolves, and so on—or even type a keyword in the search field at the bottom of the panel.

AUDIO FADES AUTOMATICALLY

When a transition is added to a video clip with attached audio, a crossfade transition is automatically applied to the audio. If the audio is detached or expanded from the video, the audio is not affected by the video transition.

ADJUST A TRANSITION

Many transitions have properties that can be modified (such as color or direction). Just select the transition in the Timeline and use the Inspector panel.

3. Skim your mouse over a transition thumbnail to see an example of what the transition looks like.

4. Apply a custom transition by selecting it and dragging it onto the edit point.

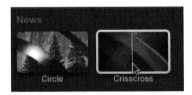

   You can also select the edit point first, and then double-click a transition in the Transitions Browser.

5. To change to a different transition, drag and drop it over the existing transition in the Timeline.

   The new transition will maintain the duration of the one it replaces.

ADD AN AUDIO CROSSFADE

There is only one type of audio transition, a cross-fade. It is important to remember that if a clip has attached audio, when you apply a video transition, a crossfade is automatically applied to the audio. On the other hand, if you apply a crossfade to the audio, the video will get a cross dissolve.

To perform an audio-only transition, you need to detach the audio from the video:

1. Right-click on a clip in the Timeline.

2. From the menu, choose Detach Audio (Control+Shift+S).

3. Once the audio and video are detached, you can apply transitions to each independently.

COPY A TRANSITION TO OTHER EDIT POINTS

If you've created a transition you like, you can easily reuse it. This will add visual consistency to your program.

To copy a transition from one edit to another:

> Press and hold the Option key, and drag the desired transition to another edit point.

> You can use the traditional copy-paste paradigm as well. Select the transition, press Command+C, select another edit in the Timeline, and press Command+V.

▲ When you detach audio, it appears as a connected clip and is semi-independent to the video. You can even select multiple clips and detach them all at the same time.

Delete Transitions from Your Project

To remove one or more transitions from your Timeline, select them and press Delete. The selected transitions are removed, and their edit points are converted to simple cuts. The duration of your program is not changed when you remove a transition.

SHOW ME A LIST OF TRANSITIONS
You can search, select, and delete transitions from the Timeline Index. This is a fast way to remove several transitions at once.

BROKEN SYNC
Detached audio runs the risk of breaking sync if moved. After applying audio crossfades, select detached video and audio components, and make a compound clip to avoid the risk.

VIDEO-ONLY TRANSITIONS
To apply a video-only transition, expand the video and audio components before applying the transition. Then collapse the audio and video components afterward.

CHAPTER 9

Fixing and Enhancing Footage

When working with video, the act of color grading and footage enhancement is generally performed at the end of the development process. The reason is that it can be a bit time-consuming, so the thought is that you should fix color, exposure, and other issues just for footage you used (as opposed to the hours you've shot).

So, once you have your cut locked down and you feel that the rhythm of the piece works, it's time to make sure your images look the best they can. Final Cut Pro X has some amazing color grading tools that allow you to fine-tune how your images look. Much like working with a photograph, the pictures that come out of the camera are not necessarily the best those images can look.

You can even use the color grading tools just to stylize the look of your program. Lots of things can influence the appearance of your footage:

> An overcast day will give you images that don't have enough contrast.

> Shooting in low light can lead to underexposed footage.

> If you have different light sources on your subject (such as daylight and fluorescent lights), your images can have different color temperatures that don't match a preset white balance.

> You may want to adjust the color balance of an image so that flesh tones look more natural.

> Color grading can also ensure that one shot matches the shot next to it, which is often called *scene-to-scene* color correction.

In addition, you can make several other types of corrections, such as compensating for shaky footage and rolling shutter, as well as making more aesthetic changes with techniques like speed changes. We'll talk about all of these corrections in this chapter.

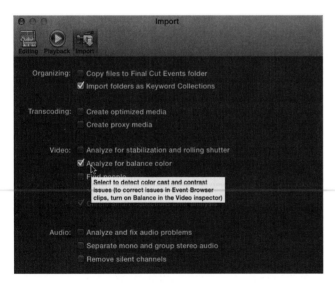

▲ Using the application's preferences, you can tell Final Cut Pro X to analyze all clips when you first import them.

IF YOU WANT TO GO DEEPER

If you want to dig deeper into the theory and nuance of color grading, a PDF called "Color Correction and Grading" is available with the book *From Still to Motion: A Photographer's Guide to Creating Video with Your DSLR* (Peachpit Press, 2010) and is also included with this book's downloaded files.

Automatic Color Correction

Final Cut Pro has a number of tools that allow you to automate many of the most common color grading and color matching chores. With a single click you can neutralize a clip's color cast and maximize an image's contrast. With two clicks you can match the look and feel of several clips in your Timeline.

Don't worry; Final Cut Pro also provides you with the ability to manually fine-tune almost every aspect of each shot. You can adjust a clip's color balance and contrast across the tonal range—shadows, midtones, and highlights. We'll explore manual adjustments later in this chapter, but for now let's focus on speed and ease.

Analyzing a Clip

When you first import a clip into your Event Library, you can have Final Cut Pro analyze the clip to determine the best adjustments to neutralize color casts and optimize contrast. This feature was touched on earlier in Chapter 3 "Importing and Transcoding Your Media," and we recommended leaving the "Analyze for balance color" check box selected. As a reminder, you will always see this dialog option whenever you import

HOW LONG WILL ANALYZING TAKE?

Analyzing a clip for color balance can take from a few seconds for shorter clips to a minute or more for longer clips. The analysis process takes longer if you also analyze for people and stabilization issues.

files, or you can select it in the Preference settings for Final Cut Pro under the Import settings. The last method is useful if you just drag and drop clips from the Finder into your project.

If you did not analyze a clip for balance color upon import, you can analyze a clip's color balance at any time in the Event Browser.

1. Select one or more clips in the Event Browser.

2. Choose Modify > Analyze and Fix.

   You can also right-click a selected clip and choose Analyze and Fix from the context menu.

3. In the new window that appears, select "Analyze for balance color."

4. Click OK.

   The clips are analyzed. Any clips that were already analyzed during import are skipped. Open the Background Tasks window to check progress.

Auto Balancing Color

Even if you've used the "Analyze for balance color" option, Final Cut Pro won't automatically adjust the clip's color balance. By default, color balance correction is turned off. You can control when to activate it, which is a good thing.

For example, perhaps you intentionally shot your footage just as the sun was setting to get that golden look. The last thing you would want is for Final Cut Pro to balance the shot and remove that beautiful golden color cast. Automatic is only useful if you choose when to engage it.

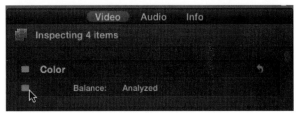

You can activate the Auto Balance on clips in either the Event Browser or the Timeline. Here's how.

1. Select the clip(s) you want to balance in the Event Browser or the Timeline.

2. If it's not already visible, open the Inspector (Command+4).

3. Select Video at the top of the Inspector.

4. Make sure the area called Color is active.

   You can tell that it's active by the blue box next to the word Color. Below that is a box labeled Balance.

5. Click the box next to Balance to activate this selection.

   The look of the selected clip(s) should change; the color casts should be lessened and the contrast enhanced. Also, notice that to the right of the word Balance is an indicator identifying whether or not the clip has been analyzed already.

SHOULD "ANALYZE FOR BALANCE COLOR" BE SELECTED?

Analyzing is a background task, so you won't see anything happening unless you open the Background Tasks window. Even though analyzing for balance color is a background task, it could still slow down the performance of your machines. Unless you know you need to balance all your shots, you may want to leave this option deselected and analyze only clips that need balancing after import.

TO ANALYZE OR NOT TO ANALYZE COLOR BALANCE

Why does it matter if you analyze a clip for color balance? When you activate the Balance option, if you haven't analyzed the clip, Final Cut Pro seems to balance it anyway. The way Final Cut balances a scene is different depending on whether or not the clip has been analyzed. If the clip has not been analyzed, Final Cut Pro will base all its color correction for that clip on the current frame, the one you see in your Viewer. If the clip has been analyzed, Final Cut Pro will use the color data from the entire clip and choose the best adjustment based on that information.

6. You can toggle Balance Color on and off from the Enhancements menu in the toolbar or by pressing Command+Option+B.

Auto Matching Color and Look

Because video projects are often shot over a long period, it's easy to get inconsistencies in your footage. For example, you might have used footage from more than one camera (especially if you were shooting a multicamera production like a concert or event). You also may have shot at different times and under different lighting conditions.

To help solve the inconsistency issue, Final Cut Pro can match your colors to smooth out variations. The Match Color feature makes it easy to ensure that all scenes that take place in the same location feel and look like they were all shot on the same camera under the same lighting conditions.

Here's how it works.

1. Select one or more clips in the Timeline that you want to match.

2. Choose Modify > Match Color (Command+Option+M). You'll also find controls in the Color section of the Video inspector.

The Viewer will change to show the Timeline playhead's frame on the right. The image on the left is what's below the pointer.

3. Skim any clip in the Timeline or the Event Browser to find a frame with the color look you want to match.

USING VISUAL REFERENCES TO MATCH COLOR

If there is a look that you want to emulate from another video or even a still image, import that media into your Event Browser and use it as a reference. You can Color Match your entire Timeline by selecting all the clips before you choose Color Match.

4. Click on the desired frame to preview that look applied to the selected clip(s).

   You can click a variety of clips until you find the look you want.

5. When you find the color match you want, click the Apply Match button in the Viewer window.

The new color balance for the clip will be based on the frame you selected. If you decide that this frame is not the best choice, simply repeat the preceding steps. You can also deactivate the Color Match by opening the Inspector and disabling the blue activation box.

Using Scopes

Final Cut Pro has a variety of video scopes that you can use as a reference when color balancing a shot or doing scene-to-scene color correction. Scopes are simply a graphical, nonsubjective way of looking at the color balance, luma, and tonality of your footage. Scopes help compensate for variation in human perception as well as the lack of consistency in how people have their computers set up.

You can get quite deep into color correction. In fact, a *colorist* is a job in the film and video world dedicated to color correcting or grading video and films. This section will give you just enough information to get you started. Again, in this book's downloads you'll find the "Color Correction and Grading" PDF from the book *From Still to Motion: A Photographer's Guide to Creating Video with Your DSLR* if you want to delve deeper.

If your program is destined for broadcast, there are also very specific limits on the maximum values of luma and chroma in each frame of your program. If a video program exceeds these limits, there can be technical issues, such as colors that bleed, but also a broadcaster can reject the program and not air it until the problems are fixed. Using the scopes to measure your luma and chroma values can help prevent these problems.

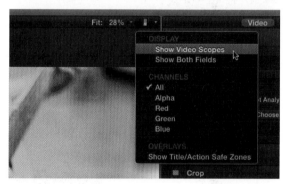

Here's how to see your video scopes (which share the same space as the Viewer).

1. In the Viewer, click the menu in the upper-right corner.

2. Choose Show Video Scopes from the Viewer Options menu or press Command+7.

   You can use the same command to hide the scopes. Only one scope appears at a time.

3. Use the Settings menu (in the upper-right corner of the scope) to switch between the three primary scopes as well as select their display options.

WAVEFORM MONITOR

The Waveform Monitor is primarily used to measure the brightness (also known as luma) of a shot. It can also be configured in a variety of ways to measure the signal. Spikes and dips in the displayed waveforms (often called the *trace*) correspond to light and dark areas in your picture. The further up the scale the trace, the brighter that portion of the image is; the closer to the bottom, the darker that part of the clip is. In essence, 0 percent represents black, whereas 100 percent represents white. The waveform also mimics the actual picture left to right.

The Settings menu in the upper-right corner of the Waveform Monitor provides a variety of display options:

> You will primarily use the Luma setting but the RGB Parade option is also very useful for measuring color balance in a clip across the tonal range (black to white).

> You can switch between IRE and millivolts. The IRE standard is more common these days, but millivolts are often used for the PAL video system.

The goal is to make sure that no parts of the image drop below 0 or exceed 100 percent on the scale. Trace between 0 and 100 percent is said to be *broadcast safe*.

As you make adjustments to the Levels of Exposure of the image, these values will update in the scope.

VECTORSCOPE

The Vectorscope shows you the overall hues as well as the saturation of those hues for a given clip. The angle of the trace around the Vectorscope indicates hue. Notice that there are six squares (targets) on the outer edge of the Vectorscope indicating the primary colors of red, green, and blue, and the secondary colors of yellow, cyan, and magenta in your image.

The distance out from center on the Vectorscope indicates saturation—trace that extends toward the outside boundaries of the scope is very saturated. If your image is black and white, the Vectorscope would show a single dot in the center of the scope to reflect the lack of color.

As a general rule, trace should never exceed the square targets. If it does, you might exceed standards by some broadcasters. Even if you're not going to broadcast a video, many devices, like DVD players and even iPads, prefer broadcast safe colors. The Vectorscope can also be used to match the color of two images that differ by acting as a reference to correct the mismatched shot.

▶ **The Waveform Monitor is a useful way to view the exposure of your image. It can help show you if an image is too bright or too dark when balancing exposure.**

HISTOGRAM

If you've worked in Photoshop, Lightroom, or Aperture, you may already be familiar with the histogram. It shows you how many black, white, and gray pixels are in your image. It also has the ability to function on a per channel basis, so as you increase the presence of color in multiple channels, new colors are visible.

It is most often used to measure the contrast of an image. Using the histogram, it's very easy to see where in the tonal range a particular lightness or color value happens. Spikes in a histogram represent more pixels of that value. Being able to spot problem areas helps you fix them. If you have a lot of spikes on the left side of your histogram, you'll notice a much darker image. If all the spikes are in the middle part of the graph, your image probably has very little contrast. Ideally, your image should look like a nice even mountain range from left to right.

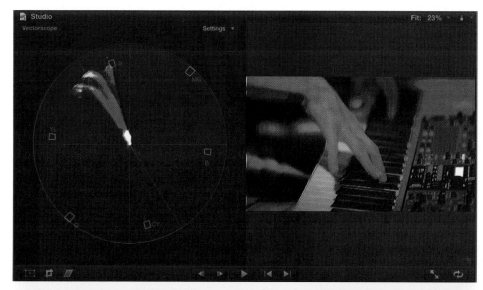

◄ The Vectorscope is a useful way to check for color cast in an image. This particular shot has a lot of red and yellow tones from stage lighting. It is also too saturated (as evident by the trace being pushed to the outer edge of the scope).

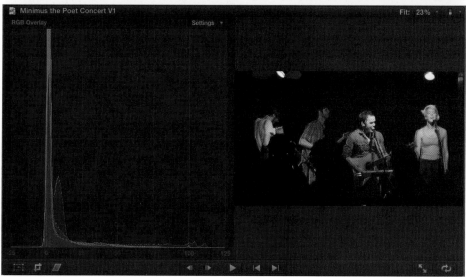

◄ The Histogram is a familiar way to view exposure and contrast in an image. It behaves similarly to the way it behaves in applications such as Photoshop, Lightroom, or Aperture.

Primary Color Correction

Now that you have a sense of what each scope is used for, let's delve into manually adjusting the color of your image. Even if you've used the Auto Balance, you may still want to refine how your image looks. Final Cut Pro allows you use both Auto Balance and manual color balancing simultaneously. You can even stack an unlimited number of color correction effects on an image to truly get the look you want.

The first step in adjusting the color of a clip is to open the color board. The color board can be accessed from the Inspector by clicking the small button to the right of Correction 1 or from the Enhancement menu

▲ The top image is the original while the lower image shows an exposure adjustment. The midtones and highlights were lifted while the shadows were pulled down to add contrast.

(Command+6). The color board is broken down into three areas that you can adjust:

> Color (Command+Control+C)
> Saturation (Command+Control+S)
> Exposure (Command+Control+E)

Let's look at each area and see how it can be used to modify the look of your image. We'll work from right to left, starting with Exposure. It's important to make contrast (exposure) adjustments first when making corrections because as you adjust contrast, you can potentially change where in the tonal range a color cast is happening.

Adjusting Exposure

When you work with the Exposure slider in Final Cut Pro, what you are really doing is adjusting the contrast. You can brighten the highlights and darken the shadows, thereby expanding the dynamic range of the clip. You ideally want the Waveform Monitor open for these adjustments because you want to be careful not to exceed 0 percent on the lower end and 100 percent on the top end.

Notice that there are four circular sliders:

> The one on the far left controls the brightness of the entire image.

> The three to the right of the main slider allow you to fine-tune luma levels in just the darkest areas (the shadows,) the midtones (similar to gamma control), and the brightest areas (the highlights).

> If the image needs a little punch, you may need to lower just the shadow area to make the black areas nice and rich.

> If a person is silhouetted, you can use the Midtones slider to raise the person's levels without causing your shadows to go gray or your highlights to blow out.

> You can use the highlight levels to bring down overly bright areas without darkening the whole image.

In the bottom half of the pane are numerical readouts that display a scale from –100% to +100%, which shows how much you've modified the clip. If you need to reset the controls back to their defaults, click the curved arrow in the upper-right corner of the pane.

Adjusting Saturation

Moving to the left are the Saturation sliders. Like Exposure, you can adjust the Saturation of the entire clip or just focus on the shadows, midtones, and highlights. There are a couple of reasons you may want to manipulate the saturation: Perhaps you just want the image to pop—in which case you might increase the Global saturation.

If you want the skin tones of people in the shot to look better but not force the whole scene's color to be more saturated, you might just work in the Midtones. Working with sliders for each part of the tonal range will give you the fine control to make a scene look its best.

▲ The lower image had saturation selectively adjusted in the tonal ranges.

Saving Correction Presets

It's a fact of life when it comes to color correction that you'll often need to use the same types of corrections over and over. This might be something as simple as needing to recall a correction to apply it to the same shot that appears repeatedly in your program, but you might also save more generic types of corrections that you find you're using over and over across different projects. For example, you might have developed a nice, saturated, warm look you can save as a preset to recall later. Here are the essential steps for saving a preset.

1. Using the built-in correction or by adding a new one, use the color board to make a correction.

2. After making the correction, a menu with a cog icon on it (Action menu) appears at the bottom of the color board. Click this menu, and then choose the first option, Save Preset.

3. In the dialog that appears, name the preset using a name germane to the correction you've made.

Just keep in mind that when you save a color correction preset, only Color, Saturation, and Exposure settings for a particular correction are saved as part of the preset. Multiple corrections would need to be saved and then reapplied separately.

Adjusting Color

Continuing to the left is the Color adjustment. It allows you to add or remove a color tint. You can adjust *the tint for the whole image* by dragging the Global control (the large gray control). And as with the previous controls, you can isolate the shadows, midtones, and highlights.

Dragging the controls up adds color to the video, and dragging them down subtracts color (effectively adding the opposite color). Dragging the controls left and right chooses the color to add or subtract.

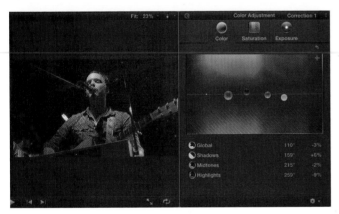

▲ By adjusting the color balance for the individual tonal ranges you can selectively adjust color spill.

SPEEDING UP COLOR CORRECTION
To reset the currently selected control to its neutral state, press Delete. To reset all of a panels controls to their neutral state, click the Reset button in the pane's upper-right corner. To reset all three color board panes back to their neutral state, in the Color section of the Video inspector, click the Reset button to the right of the Correction setting. If the clip has multiple corrections applied to it, choose the correction to adjust from the Correction menu in the color board's upper-right corner.

Secondary Color Correction

Now that we've taken a look at the essentials of primary color correction—corrections that affect the entire clip—let's switch gears and talk about secondary color correction in Final Cut Pro X. Secondary corrections target a specific portion of the image.

For example, you might have a shot in which everything looks great but someone's skin tone is a little red. By using a secondary color correction, you could target only the skin tone of the person in the shot, leaving other portions of the clip untouched.

Final Cut Pro X provides two ways to make secondary color corrections: using a Color Mask and using a Shape Mask. We'll explore both methods in this section.

Using Color Masks

We'll admit it; when we first heard the term Color Mask, we were a little confused about what it was. But after actually using a Color Mask, we quickly realized that it was just like what other applications call a *key*, specifically an HSL key (Hue, Saturation, and Lightness).

Color Masks are great for targeting things like skin tone and skies to treat them in a stylistic way. But they're also a great tool to use when you're trying to select a portion of a clip to reduce, for example, brightness or saturation while trying to maintain broadcast legality.

Here's how to use a Color Mask.

1. With a shot selected, open the Inspector and click the Video tab.

2. Next to the word Color, click the plus button to add an additional correction.

Remember that all clips have one correction already applied to them. Use this first correction for the primary correction and add additional corrections for secondary corrections.

3. Locate the two icons to the right of the new correction you just added.

4. Click the eyedropper to add a Color Mask.

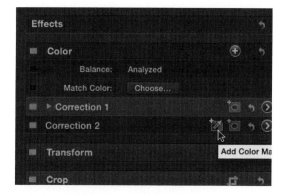

When you click the Color Mask button, the cursor changes to an eyedropper.

5. In the Viewer, click and drag slightly but don't release your mouse button yet.

As you drag, you'll notice a set of two circles as you drag out. As the circles get bigger, you'll be making a larger selection of HSL values. The smaller the circles, the more exacting the selection. Also as you drag, the Viewer changes to a desaturated hybrid view, meaning that what you've selected with the eyedropper will be in color or saturated and portions of the footage that aren't selected will be desaturated or in grayscale. This makes it very easy to see what you've selected.

After you've made a selection, you'll see a color swatch with your selected color appear under the name of the new correction. Next to this is a slider that controls the softness of the selection you've made.

6. Adjust the softness setting so that when you make the actual correction, you won't have any ringing edges. This creates a gradual transition between the corrected and uncorrected areas.

▲ The exposure in the face was adjusted using a color mask.

7. Making the selection is only part of the process when it comes to using Color Masks. Now that you've made a selection, click the Show Correction button (the right-facing arrow on a color wheel).

8. Using the Color, Saturation, and Exposure (contrast) tabs, make the correction that you need. As you do, you'll notice that the correction affects only the selection that you've made, leaving the rest of the clip untouched.

One nice feature when making a correction using Color Masks in Final Cut Pro X is that when you're using a Color Mask, at the bottom portion of the color board, when it's showing Color, Saturation, and Exposure controls, are two buttons for Inside Mask and Outside Mask. Using these two controls, you can choose whether your correction is affecting the portion of the clip you selected with the eyedropper (Inside Mask) or the portions you didn't select (Outside Masks). By using these controls, you can essentially make two secondary corrections with one selection of the Color Mask eyedropper.

Using Shape Masks

Although Color Masks can be very useful in many situations, in some situations they don't work particularly well (especially if there are too many similar HSL values in a clip to make a clean selection).

Another tool that we just love is a Shape Mask. A Shape Mask, also called a vignette or window in other applications, lets you use a geometric shape to make a correction. Shape Masks are particularly useful for tasks like relighting a shot—brightening someone's face, for example, while darkening other parts of the clip to focus a viewer's attention toward the face. Shape Masks can be used in a variety of other situations as well.

Let's take a look at adding Shape Masks in Final Cut Pro X.

1. With a shot selected, open the Inspector and click the Video tab.

2. Next to the word Color, click the plus button to add an additional correction.

3. Locate the two icons to the right of the new correction you just added.

4. Click the second icon with the plus button in the upper-left corner with a circle in the center to add a Shape Mask.

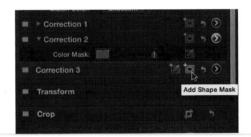

THEORY AND APPLICATION
If you're eager to learn more about color theory and how that theory is applied in color correction applications by professional colorists, check out our colleague Alexis Van Hurkman's excellent book *Color Correction Handbook: Professional Techniques for Video and Cinema* (Peachpit Press, 2010).

5. After you add a Shape Mask, the Viewer will display two circles. The default shape is a circle, but using the onscreen controls you can easily manipulate the shape.

   Notice the four green dots around the inside circle. Dragging these dots allows you to resize and change the aspect of the shape to better fit the object you're trying to isolate onscreen.

6. Near the topmost green dot is a smaller dot to the left. Dragging this dot allows you to change the shape from a circle to more of a square.

7. After choosing the type of shape you want and adjusting sizing and aspect, clicking in the center of the shape on the large circle at the very center allows you to reposition the shape. With the handle (the line with another circle at the end) attached to this center circle, you can rotate the shape.

8. Clicking and dragging the outside circle allows you adjust the softness of the shape. It's important to add a bit of softness anytime you use a Shape Mask; otherwise, the edges of the shape will be visible in the final shot.

9. To actually make a correction, click the Show Correction button to reveal the color board.

Depending on what you're trying to do, you can make Color, Saturation, or Exposure corrections. And as with Color Masks, you can make corrections inside the shape (Inside Mask) or outside the shape (Outside Mask) by using the two buttons at the bottom of the color board. So, using the relighting a scene example at the start of this section, you'd lighten inside the shape and then switch to Outside Mask and darken the outside of the shape.

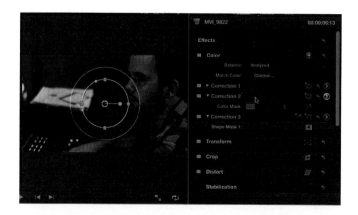

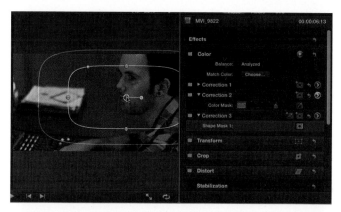

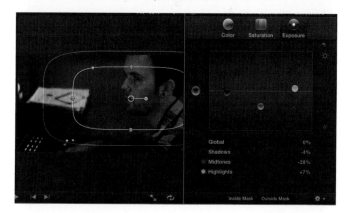

▲ The initial shape was added (top). The shape was then adjusted using the handles and then was repositioned over the subject's face (center). An exposure adjustment was then applied to darken the edges (bottom).

KEYFRAMING SHAPE MASKS
When you start using Shape Masks, you'll quickly get addicted to how useful they are. However, they have one downside: When the object that you've placed in a Shape Mask moves, the shape doesn't. That's OK! After you add a Shape Mask to a correction, in the Inspector you can use the Keyframe menu for the Shape Mask to animate it onscreen.

Combining Color and Shape Masks

Sometimes there are situations when color grading in which only a Color Mask will work to make the correction you need to make. However, when you use a Color Mask, often additional portions of the shot are selected that you don't want selected. That's OK! By combining Color and Shape Masks, you can essentially "limit" the selection by a Color Mask to the area inside the shape.

1. With a shot selected, open the Inspector and click the Video tab.

2. Next to the word Color, click the plus button to add an additional correction.

3. Add a Color Mask, but drag out quite a bit to make a larger selection than is needed.

4. Show the correction for the Color Mask and use the color board to make a correction. You should notice that your correction affects more than just the portions of the clip you wanted to affect.

5. From the color board, click the Back button (upper-left corner of the color board).

6. On the same correction that you previously added to make the Color Mask, click the icon to create a Shape Mask.

   When you do, you'll notice that a shape was created. Adjust the mask as needed.

   The correction that you previously made by using a Color Mask is limited to the inside of the shape. Further refine the adjustment to taste.

Other Corrections

Although you'll do color correction all the time, there are other common types of corrections that you can make to footage in Final Cut Pro X to make your footage look its best. Shaky footage or the bending of straight lines due to a DSLR's rolling shutter can drive

◄ A mask selection based on color (top). The addition of a shape mask further isolates the selection (middle images). A localized exposure adjustment (bottom) adjusts exposure on just the face of the guitar.

you (and potentially your clients) crazy! Fortunately, Final Cut Pro X has some very cool and useful tools to help with these types of fixes. In this section we'll take a quick peek at these tools.

Stabilizing Footage

Unless you're shooting a *Bourne Identity* style action film, you'll probably not want your footage to look like the camera operator was intoxicated. If you do end up with shaky footage, Final Cut Pro X can help. Similar to using the Balance Color option discussed earlier in this chapter to stabilize footage, you first need to analyze the clip, which can be done in two ways:

> **On import.** When importing footage from disk, one of the options you have in the Video section of the Import Files dialog is to "Analyze for stabilization and rolling shutter" on import. If you choose this option, clips will be analyzed in the background and most likely the analyzing will be done by the time you're ready to stabilize or repair rolling shutter (discussed next).

> **Activating Stabilization in the Inspector.** If you didn't choose to analyze a clip for stabilization on import, simply select the clip and then choose Stabilization from the Inspector (it's on the Video pane of the main Inspector). When you enable stabilization, analyzing will begin in the background.

After a clip has been analyzed for movement, you can then use the Translation (think position up/down, left/right), Rotation, and Scale smoothness parameters to fine-tune the amount of stabilization you require for a shot.

Repairing Rolling Shutter

Shooting with a video-enabled DSLR, you've probably become familiar with the phenomenon of rolling shutter. Rolling shutter results from the way CMOS image sensors scan. Rolling shutter can especially result when there are quick lateral movements in a shot, and rolling shutter is most evident in normally straight vertical lines being bent during these movements. An

▲ The Stabilization option offers 3 levels of control. The more you increase the smoothness settings, the more the image must be scaled.

▲ Rolling shutter works to repair bending in an image caused by fast pans or movement.

awesome feature in Final Cut Pro X compensates for rolling shutter. As when stabilizing footage, the clip needs to be analyzed first. And similar to stabilizing footage, you can accomplish this stabilization in the same two ways.

After activating rolling shutter compensation and analysis is complete, there are no further controls to manipulate. Final Cut Pro X will do its best to alleviate rolling shutter artifacts.

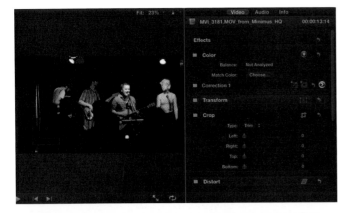

▲ An image can be cropped in several ways. The Inspector (top) uses sliders and numerical values. You can use the Trim option (middle) to remove footage from the visible frame, but gaps are left behind. The Crop option (bottom) constrains the cropping to match the footage's aspect ratio. It also scales the image larger to remove any gaps.

Cropping Footage

Although not a correction in the same sense that, say, a color correction or stabilization is, often you'll need to crop clips to get rid of unsightly items in the frame, like a boom mic or something similar. You can also of course crop for atheistic reasons. There are two main ways to crop in Final Cut Pro X:

> **From the Inspector.** Select a clip, navigate to the Inspector, and locate the Transform parameter. If it's not already enabled (default), you can enable it by clicking the box to the left of the parameter. The parameter is on when the box is blue. From there you choose to "Show" the crop controls (the blue text next to the crop icon).

> **In the Viewer.** There are two ways to enable cropping in the Viewer. First, from the Inspector, enable the Crop parameter, and then click the Crop icon to the right of the word Crop. You'll notice a bounding box or wireframe in the Viewer. Second, press Shift+C. Regardless of how you activate cropping in the Viewer, you can use the onscreen controls (the blue handles on the corners of the bounding box) to actually crop the clip.

When cropping in Final Cut Pro X, there are a few different types of crops that you can use:

> **Trim.** This crop type allows you to do what its name implies, which is trim any side of the clip. After you trim, portions of the clip will be cut off or trimmed and the resulting black area becomes transparent. If you're using the controls in the Inspector, you'll see your results as you adjust the controls. If you're using the onscreen controls in the Viewer, when you click Done, the shot will be cropped and reframed.

THE DANGERS OF CROPPING
Video is a very low-resolution medium. Keep in mind that when you crop video, you are essentially blowing up the image. This will lead to softening. Try not to crop too tightly, and of course, shooting it right the first time is always the best option.

> **Crop.** This crop type works the same way that other applications—like Adobe Photoshop—work by either using the onscreen controls in the Viewer or the Crop parameter in the Inspector to reframe the shot to your liking. If you're using the controls in the Inspector, you'll see your results as you adjust the controls. If you're using the onscreen controls in the Viewer, when you click Done, the shot will be cropped and reframed.

> **Ken Burns.** Named after the iconic documentary filmmaker who popularized movement on photos, this crop type must be done in the Viewer with the onscreen controls because there are no parameters to adjust in the Inspector. In the Viewer, when this crop type is selected, you'll see two bounding boxes—a green box for the start framing of the clip and a red box for the end framing of the clip. Using the onscreen controls, you can frame the clip however you'd like for the start and end of the clip. As you move the boxes, an arrow will show you the movement that will result because of the reframing or cropping. After you click Done in the Viewer, Final Cut Pro X will automatically animate the clip for the different framing.

Mixing Formats in Your Timeline

As you edit a project, you may find that you're mixing frame rates and even resolutions into the same project. From the strictest technical sense, this is not ideal because it means the differing assets will need to be converted to match the rest of the footage used (a process called *conforming*). Fortunately, Final Cut Pro X does a good job conforming footage.

Conforming is driven by your project settings, so if you change the codec or frame rate of your project, clips that do not match are conformed. You can also conform an individual clip and even change how the process occurs.

Here are a few rules to remember:

> The original video and audio project properties should match how you want to share the movie with an audience. For example, if you intend to publish for television, you'll likely set your project's video properties to 1080p HD.

> Although you can change a project's frame size at any time, changing its frame rate can wreak havoc. All the edit points in your project will shift in time when the rate setting is changed. Avoid this at all costs.

> The first clip you added to a project should match the video and audio properties in which you intend to share your project. We discussed this in depth in Chapter 5, "Setting Up a Project."

Conforming Frame Size

So what happens when the size of your footage differs from the output you've chosen? By default, Final Cut Pro modifies the frame size of any nonmatching clips to match the project's frame size settings.

Here's how you can control this conversion.

1. Select a clip in the Timeline whose frame size doesn't match the current project's frame size (resolution) settings.

2. Click the Inspector button in the toolbar to open the Video inspector.

3. Choose a method for conforming the frame size from the Type menu in the Spatial Conform section of the Video inspector:

> **Fit.** This is the default setting. The clip is fit within the project's frame size without any cropping. If the aspect ratios of the clips match (such as putting 720p footage into a 1080 composition), the conversion is difficult to detect. In the case of mixing HD and SD footage, you may end up with black bars next to the image (this is often referred to as *letterboxing* or *pillarboxing*).

> **Fill.** This option scales a clip so it fills the project's frame size. The Fill option always leads to cropping when the aspect ratios differ between clip and project. This option scales the image the most and can lead to visible softening.

> **None.** This option tells Final Cut Pro X to leave the clip's frame size unchanged. For clips that are larger than the project, they will appear cropped. For smaller clips, they will be padded with black bars surrounding the clip.

Conforming Frame Rate

When you mix frame rates, Final Cut Pro employs a frame-sampling method to the clips that doesn't match the project settings. Frames must either be added or deleted from the clips to preserve the playback speed. Otherwise, you may end up with unintended motion effects. Final Cut Pro X offers four methods to choose from. The amount of visual stuttering and artifacts varies depending on which method you choose.

You can choose which frame-sampling method Final Cut Pro uses by following these steps.

1. Select a clip in the Timeline whose frame rate doesn't match the current project's frame rate settings.

2. Click the Inspector button in the toolbar to open the Video inspector.

3. Choose a method for conforming the frame rate from the Frame Sampling menu in the Rate Conform section of the Video inspector:

> **Floor.** This is the default setting. Frames are discarded or duplicated to match the project's frame rate. This method is fast but not very high quality.

> **Nearest Neighbor.** This method is similar to the Floor method but reduces artifacts in the image. It does, however, have the tendency to add visual stuttering. Rendering is required for this method.

> **Frame Blending.** This is the most common method used by discerning pros. New in-between frames are created by blending individual pixels of neighboring frames. This works very well for slow motion clips as well as when dramatic differences exist between project and clip frame rates (such as when mixing 24p material into a 29.97 project). This setting reduces visual stuttering, but you may see some visual artifacts. Rendering is required for this method.

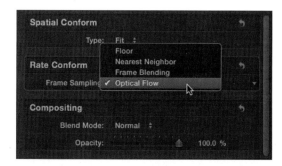

> **Optical Flow.** This is the highest-quality method offered by Final Cut Pro X. New frames are created using an optical flow algorithm that generates frames by morphing between two frames to make a clean new frame. This produces excellent results with little to no visual stuttering or artifacts. However, with quality comes cost. Final Cut Pro spends a significant amount of rendering, which is required for this method.

Retiming Footage

Retiming footage in the editorial process is just as common as making a trim; it's something that you'll need to do all the time. You might change the speed of a clip for aesthetic reasons if you want an action to happen faster or slower. You might also change the speed of a clip to reverse action or to have a clip fit a specific period of time. You might even want to stop action altogether and create what's known as a freeze frame (essentially a still where you can control the duration). Regardless of the reason, changing the speed of clips is easy.

Changing Clip Speed

Changing the speed of a clip in Final Cut Pro X is very straightforward. You can create clips that are slower or clips that are faster, and you can even perform a variable speed change where a clip ramps between high speed and slow motion and back to normal speed (you see this effect in movies and commercials all the time).

There are a few ways to change the speed of a clip; each one involves first selecting the clip whose speed you want to change:

> **Retime menu.** With a clip selected, simply click the Retime menu (the icon looks like a speedometer on the right side of the screen). From this menu you can choose to slow down or speed up a clip. You can also choose to ramp the speed change of a clip from 0 to 100 percent or vice versa. There are some pretty cool presets to provide Instant Replay and Rewind Effects.

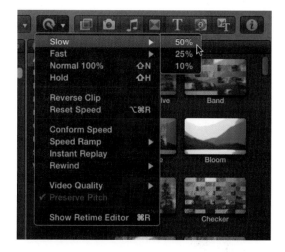

> **From the Timeline.** If you change the speed properties of a clip from the Retime menu, you'll notice that a Retiming section appears above the clip on the Timeline. Using the controls in this section, you can manipulate the speed of a clip. You can also select a clip you want to retime in the Timeline and press Command+R.

Once you have revealed the retiming bar, it is quite easy to adjust a clip's speed to your specific needs. Here are some essentials:

> **Speed menu on a clip.** If you use the Retime menu to change the speed of a clip, you'll notice that the Retiming bar that appears above the clip will be one of four colors. If the clip is playing back faster, the bar will be blue; if the clip is playing back slower, the bar will be orange; and if

▲ The Speed Ramp options can also be used to create a transition from paused to full-speed action.

you created a freeze (hold) frame, the bar will be red. If the bar is green, the clip is playing back at 100 percent.

> If you want to modify the speed further in the Timeline, you can click the triangle next to the percentage of speed. You'll then have some of the same options, like slowing down and speeding up a clip, that are available from the Retiming menu on the main interface.

> **Trimming to refine speed changes.** You've probably noticed that in both the Retiming menu and the drop-down menus, your choices for speeding up or slowing down a clip are rather limited to three or four fixed options. Don't despair. Look closely at the right side of the Retiming bar above the clip and you'll notice a handle (double bars). By clicking and dragging this handle to the right, you can slow down the clip incrementally; by dragging to the left, you can speed up the clip incrementally.

> **Creating speed segments.** Sometimes you'll want to create speed changes within a clip. For example, you might want to start a clip playing at 100 percent, then slow it down to 40 percent, and then speed it back up to 100 percent. These types of effects are easy to create. In the Tools menu select the Range Selection tool or press R. Then simply drag to highlight the section of the clip you'd like to change the speed of. Keep in mind that after making the initial selection, you can place your cursor at either end of the selection and trim to refine the selection. If the whole clip is accidentally selected, press the

Shift key to grab anywhere you want in the middle of the clip. After making the selection, head over to the Retime menu on the main interface and choose to speed up or slow down the selection. You can also do this to a clip that already has speed adjustments applied. The really cool thing is that Final Cut Pro X will automatically ramp speed between the sections to create a smooth transition.

There are two more important details to keep in mind when changing speeds in Final Cut Pro X:

> Changing the speed of clips can change the timing of your program because clips get longer or shorter.

> If you completely mess up a clip by playing with retiming, just reset the clip back to 100 percent.

REFINING SPEED SEGMENTS
After creating a speed segment, you'll notice that on the right side of the Retiming bar are handles (double bars) that you can drag to retime the segment further.

BEING PRECISE ABOUT LAST FRAME OF SPEED SEGMENT
If you need to be precise about the last frame of a speed segment, simply click the menu for that segment and choose Change End Source Frame. When you do, a filmstrip icon will appear between the speed segments. You can then drag the filmstrip icon to the left or right to choose the exact end frame of the segment while maintaining the overall speed of the segment.

Speed Change Quality

When you're doing any type of speed change with Final Cut Pro, there is an important option to pay attention to—the video quality of the speed change. After you've made a speed change, if you click the Retiming menu on the main part of the interface, one of the options you have is Video Quality. From there you can choose three different options:

> **Normal.** This option will repeat frames when slowing down a clip. This is the default method. Depending on the source footage and the amount that you're changing the speed of a clip, this option can make footage look a little jerky. We don't generally recommend this option.

> **Frame Blending.** This option blends frames together to create a smoother change of motion. Think of it as mini dissolves between each frame. This option will take a little longer to process, but the results are often much better than the Normal option.

> **Optical Flow.** If you don't mind waiting longer for processing, Optical Flow is the best choice to make, particularly when creating slow motion. It morphs changes between frames, literally creating new pixels based on their current position and motion vectors to create beautiful slow motion effects.

Reverse Clips

Reversing the action in a clip in Final Cut Pro is very simple. You'll often need to reverse for continuity purposes. For example, perhaps the camera panned left and you needed a pan right. As long as there are no people walking or some other type of movement that would look weird in reverse in the shot, you are OK. To reverse a clip, simply use the following procedure.

1. Select a clip from the Timeline.

2. Navigate to the Retiming menu on the main part of the interface.

3. From the Retiming menu, choose the option to reverse the clip.

After choosing to reverse a clip, you'll see the Retiming section above the clip on the Timeline. Notice on the green bar that it shows Reverse Normal (−100%). This indicates that the clip is running in reverse.

As with normal speed changes, you can continue to manipulate the speed change by dragging the handle at the right side of the Retiming bar (the double bars) and dragging left or right to speed up or slow down the reverse action.

Creating Freeze (Hold) Frames

Freeze frames, or stills of action, from video footage are very useful. Sometimes you'll want to hold or "freeze" on a particular action or maybe just create a still of a particular part of a video clip. Either way, creating a freeze frame with Final Cut Pro X is pretty easy. Let's explore how.

1. With the Select tool, if you have skimming enabled (S), click on the frame of a clip you want to make a freeze frame.

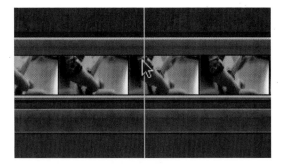

If you don't have skimming enabled, simply drag the playhead to the frame you want to freeze. Using the left and right arrow keys or zooming in to greater detail on the Timeline really helps in selecting the best frame.

2. Either click the Retiming menu and choose Hold, or press Shift+H.

3. After choosing to create a hold, you'll notice on the clip that there is a segment in deep red that shows Hold (0%). This is the hold frame or freeze frame.

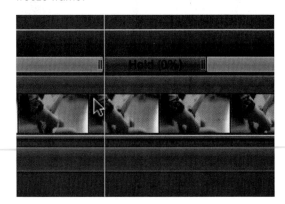

The default duration of a freeze or hold frame is two seconds. However, you can change the duration of the hold frame by dragging the handle (double bars) on right of the hold/freeze section and dragging left or right to shorten or lengthen its duration.

Color Correction on a Computer Monitor—Better Use Scopes!

Television and computer monitors can be set up differently from each other. As a matter of fact, TVs display colors very differently than computer monitors. HD video even has a standard called *Rec 709* (there are some other standards, but Rec 709 is the most widely used) that specifies how color and contrast are displayed (officially, Rec 709 is ITU-R Bt.709 and is named after the standards body that created it). Your computer monitor cannot accurately display color and contrast according to what the Rec 709 spec calls for.

This is the reason many edit suites and all color correction suites use dedicated, calibrated broadcast monitors. By making decisions about color and contrast on a calibrated display that adheres to Rec 709, you can be sure that the corrections you make are accurate.

If you make corrections using a noncalibrated computer monitor, your program might look differently when viewed on a TV. For example, on a TV, light gray looks pure white, reds are more saturated, and browns tend to be a bit more yellow. (As of this writing, external monitoring [the ability to interface with a calibrated display] in Final Cut Pro X is in its infancy, but work by Apple and third parties is in progress.)

As a result, you'll have to do a lot of color correction on your computer monitor, and for that reason, you can't really trust your monitor. Therefore, you should instead trust the video scopes. The scopes provide exact measurements of the luma and chroma levels of your clips so that you can make more informed decisions about adjusting Final Cut Pro color correction settings.

▲ A viewfinder or loupe is a useful way to gauge color and exposure while shooting.

CHAPTER 10

Working with Audio

Talk to experienced video editors and

they'll tell you that audio is half the picture. What they really mean is that a good sound track is at least as important as the visual. Without good sound, most people will stop watching even the most compelling visuals.

You'll find that Final Cut Pro X has a robust set of audio tools. You can mix and filter your audio to create the best sound possible. You can also record audio directly into the application for narration. Let's explore several ways to enhance the audio in your projects.

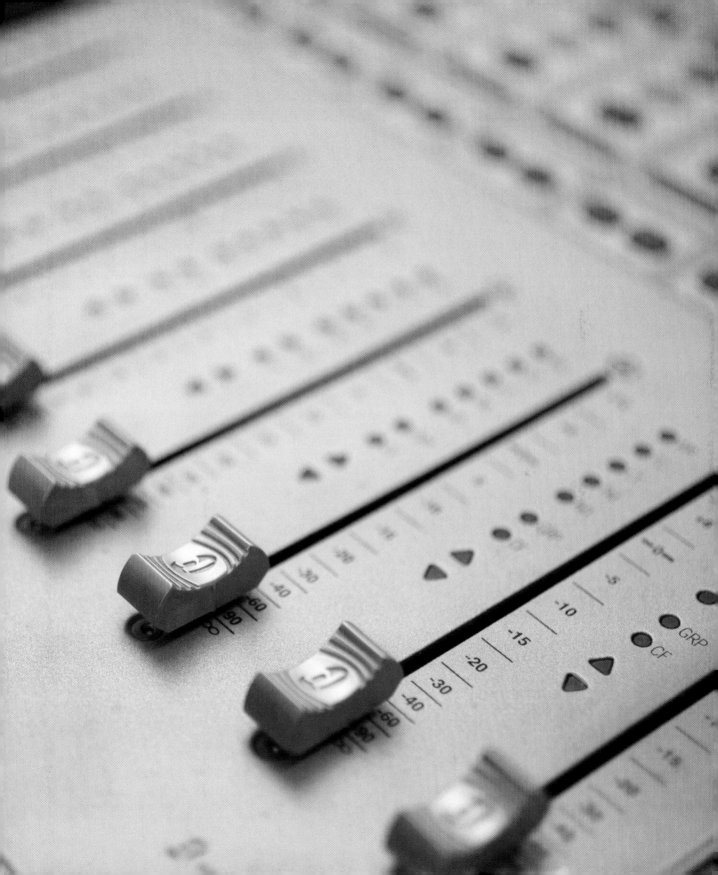

Add Music or Sound Effects

Adding music or sound effects to your project is very similar to other media types, like photos or footage. You can import them into an Event (like any other asset) and organize the media with keywords for ease of use. You can also add the content to iTunes and let it manage the assets.

Let's explore the Music and Sound Browser:

1. Click the Music and Sound button in the toolbar.

   You'll find a number of folders that include built-in sound effects. The number will vary depending on what other software is installed on your computer. You can also click iTunes to browse your music library or GarageBand to hear songs you've created and shared to the Media Browser.

2. Choose a category folder in the top area of the window.

   A new list of choices appears at the bottom of the Browser. You can also click the disclosure triangle (if available) to see categories within the folder.

3. Browse the list to locate the sound you want.

   › To search for an item, enter text in the search field.

   › To filter the list, click the Filter button and choose a category.

   › To preview a song, double-click its name.

4. Click once to select a song or Command-click to select more than one item.

5. Drag the sound file(s) to your Event or Timeline.

6. Click the close button at the top of the Browser when you're finished to close it and make more room for your Timeline.

▲ Click the Music and Sound button to open the corresponding browser or choose Window > Browser > Music and Sound.

CUSTOMIZE THE MUSIC AND SOUND BROWSER

If you don't find the sounds that you're looking for in the Music and Sound Browser, just drag a folder of audio files in from the Finder or desktop to the Music and Sound Browser.

THE OPTION TO JUST USE THE AUDIO

If you press Option+3, your Connect, Insert, and Append Media buttons will switch to only using the audio of the selected clip in the Event Browser. You can press Option+2 to switch to video only or Option+1 to use both video and audio.

Viewing Audio Clips

When working with audio, it often becomes necessary to refine your view. This is often the case when creating a final audio mix because you want to see the waveforms as well as the audio meters so you can ensure that the audio file is not clipping. It can also come in handy as you try to perform audio repairs to remove or minimize problem areas.

Understanding Waveforms

The information you see in the Timeline about an audio clip is called a *waveform*. This visual representation shows you details about the actual sound. When working with audio in a Timeline, you have several ways to

interact with the audio waveforms. You can zoom in or out to see details, or you can make the waveform taller or shorter.

Audio waveforms will display in your Timeline in two ways:

> Waveforms that reference audio attached to a video clip are blue.

> Waveforms that reference a detached or audio-only clip are green.

You can often spot details in an audio waveform by learning to read them. For example, a narrow spike in an audio waveform could be the clapboard that you used for sync sound. You can also spot gaps in an interview where the waveforms become shorter, which indicates when an off-camera question was being asked of the subject.

When you make a change to an audio clip in the Timeline, the waveform actually changes. For example, if you made a clip louder by increasing the volume, the waveforms would become taller. With time and experience, you'll quickly learn to depend on this important data to help find edit points.

NEED A REFERENCE POINT?
You can turn on a second set of waveforms to compare your original audio to the adjusted audio. Simply choose Final Cut Pro > Preferences and in the Editing tab select the option "Show reference waveforms."

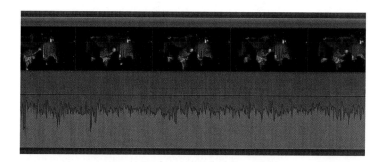

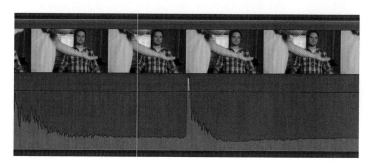

◄ The large, sharp spike is the sound of hands clapping for audio sync. The rise in the waveform at the left edge is background conversation off mic.

Show Expanded Audio and Video

When you normally view a video clip with audio, the audio display is fairly small. One important viewing method to know is how to view audio and video separately. This is called *expanding* a clip. This is also an essential view if you've created a split edit because it's the only way to see overlapping waveforms. Here's how to expand a clip:

> You can expand a single clip by double-clicking its audio waveform.

> You can select one or more clips in the Timeline and choose Clip > Expand Audio/Video (Control+S).

> You can expand all clips in the Timeline by choosing View > Expand Audio/Video Clips, and then choose For All (to see every clip) or For Split (to just see split edits). The expanded audio always stays attached to its original video.

Collapsing Audio and Video

Once you've expanded an audio/video view, you'll want to know how to switch it back. The process is virtually identical:

> You can collapse a single clip by double-clicking its audio waveform.

> You can select one or more clips in the Timeline and choose Clip > Collapse Audio/Video (Control+S).

> You can collapse all clips in the Timeline by choosing View > Collapse All Clips.

Detach Audio from Video

When you import a video clip with audio, Final Cut Pro treats it as one clip by default. There will be times when you'll only want to use the audio on a clip (such as a background sound effect for ambient noise).

Although expanding and collapsing are useful, you may want a more permanent change. If you want to create a separate audio file (that's still connected), you can also detach the audio file by choosing Clip > Detach Audio (Control+Shift+S). This will create a new audio clip that is connected beneath the video clip. You can then drag the clip to reposition it as needed.

▲ Expanding the audio and video tracks can make it easier to see waveforms (as well as make audio only adjustments).

▲ By detaching the audio from the b-roll clip, it will be easier to adjust the background noise levels and mix its levels (as you'll learn later in the chapter).

USE THE PRECISION EDITOR
You learned about trimming and detailed feedback in Chapter 8. The Precision Editor is another way to see a detached view of the audio.

NOT SEEING AUDIO WAVEFORMS?
If your Timeline isn't displaying audio waveforms, they might be hidden. Click the Appearance button in the lower-right corner of the application and choose an option that includes waveforms. You can also adjust the height to see more audio detail.

Mixing Audio

As you build your Timeline in Final Cut Pro X, you'll end up with several audio files. Some will be attached to video clips in the primary storyline; others may be attached to b-roll shots or exist as music and sound effects audio-only clips. All of these offer precise controls so you can balance the audio and create a compelling overall mix.

Using Audio Meters

As you work with audio in your Timeline, you'll need to measure and evaluate the changes. The reason is that the audio can actually be "too loud." If the overall sound levels add up to a cumulative mix that is "hot," you could hear distortion as well as clicks or pops in the sound track.

View Audio Waveforms in Greater Detail

When you truly become experienced with editing audio, you'll want more control. When it comes to trimming an unwanted "umm" or a cough, you'll need greater control than frame-based viewing. In this case you can switch to viewing your audio at the audio sample level.

To enable this view, choose Final Cut Pro > Preferences. Then click the Time Display menu and choose the second option, HH:MM:SS:FF + Subframes.

You can then see audio samples at a fraction of a second (for example, 1/48,000 for audio recorded at a sample rate of 48 kHz). This will work for connected audio clips (outside the primary storyline) or compound clips that contain only audio. You'll still receive a benefit with this method for video clips because you can now zoom to a magnitude of 1/80 the duration of a video frame.

Here's how to enable subframe viewing.

1. Choose View > Zoom to Samples (Control+Z).

2. Select a clip in your Timeline.

3. Zoom in until the clip shows the waveform detail that you want. You can press Command+= or Command+- to zoom in and out.

4. Make any edits to the audio (more on that later in this chapter).

   › To move backward in one-subframe increments, press Command+left arrow.

   › To move forward in one-subframe increments, press Command+right arrow.

5. When you're done, you can turn off zooming by choosing View > Zoom to Samples (Control+Z).

 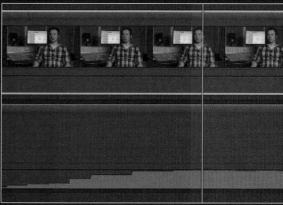

▲ The image shows the maximum standard zoom. Choosing View > Zoom to Samples makes it easier to see audio waveforms and make finer adjustments.

By default, a small set of audio meters is always displayed in the Dashboard. Here's how to open larger audio meters:

> Choose Window > Show Audio Meters.

> Click the Audio Meter icon in the Dashboard in the toolbar.

> Press Command+Shift+8 to toggle visibility.

> You can also drag the left edge of the Audio Meters to resize them.

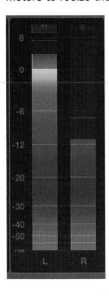

◀ Be sure to keep an eye (and an ear) open to spot audio distortion caused by clipping.

We prefer to leave these open at all times, but you can hide them if you change your mind:

> Choose Window > Hide Audio Meters.

> Click the Audio Meter icon in the Dashboard in the toolbar.

> Press Command+Shift+8 to toggle visibility.

To see the audio meters in action, select a clip in an Event or in your Timeline and click Play. The bouncing lines indicate the audio levels. If the audio clip is approaching peak levels during playback, the color changes from green to yellow (warning you that you are getting close to the threshold). If a clip exceeds peak levels, the level color changes from yellow to red. Another visual sign is that the peak indicator lights turn

red for the offending audio channel or channels. These lights will stay red until you stop and restart playback.

What should you do? That's simple. Lower the volume for those offending clips. How much should you adjust the volume? Well, that depends on your delivery:

> Broadcast average levels are –20 dB with peaks of –10 dB.

> Non-broadcast average levels are –12 dB with peaks of –3 dB.

> Web average levels are –12 dB with peaks of –1 dB.

Remember that if you hit 0 dB, your audio has distortion. The reason that broadcast levels are so conservative is that the video signal gets routed through many transceivers and components as it gets delivered via satellite or cable.

Soloing Audio Clips

One of the most useful features of Final Cut Pro X when mixing audio is the solo feature. If you solo a clip or a selection of clips, the rest of the items in the Timeline are temporarily disabled. This comes in handy when you want to isolate a clip to make adjustments (for example, you might want to hear dialogue without music to properly adjust effects and levels).

1. Select one or more clips in your Timeline.

2. To solo the selected items, do *one* of the following:

   > Click the Solo button in the Timeline.

   > Choose Clip > Solo (Option+S).

   The soloed clip is highlighted, and all other clips are dimmed to a gray color.

3. Listen to the soloed clip to evaluate the audio.

4. Make any adjustments to the soloed clip.

   You'll learn more techniques throughout this chapter.

5. To return the Timeline to normal, just remove the solo. Click the Solo button or choose Clip > Solo again.

▲ The image on the left shows all clips active, whereas the image on the right shows the audio clip soloed.

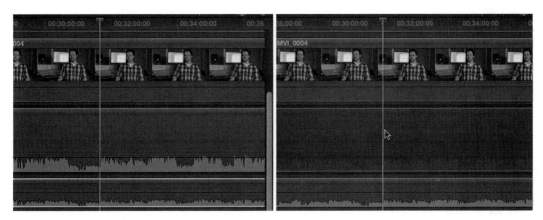

▲ The image on the left shows all clips active, whereas the image on the right shows the audio clip muted.

Muting Audio Clips

Although soloing is a temporary state (that you toggle on and off), there is another way to silence a clip. You can turn off a clip so it is disabled. This means that the clip's video portions become invisible and its audio becomes silent. A disabled (muted) clip will also not appear in any file you output.

1. Select one or more clips in your Timeline.

2. Choose Clip > Disable or press the shortcut V.

   If a clip is disabled, it will be silent and appear dimmed in the Timeline.

3. If you want to reenable a disabled clip, reselect it in the Timeline and press V.

Configuring Channels

When you first imported your audio files, Final Cut Pro X assigned a default channel configuration. Some audio formats should stay as a stereo pair (such as music). Other times you'll have a camera clip that is really two mono clips. For example, it is common practice to run a subject's lavaliere microphone to one channel and a boom mic to the other. In this case you can change the channel configuration as needed:

> **Mono.** A single channel. In most cases a mono clip is centered to come out equally through both speakers in a stereo pair.

> **Stereo.** Left and right audio channels.

> **5.1 surround.** Left, center, right, left surround, right surround, and low-frequency (subwoofer bass) channels.

> **7.1 surround.** Left, center, right, left surround, right surround, left back, right back, and low-frequency (subwoofer bass) channels.

The choices available will be based on your source clip. For most DSLR productions, your choices will be limited to Stereo or Mono.

Here's how to modify a clip.

1. Select a clip in your Timeline or in an Event.

2. Open the Inspector (Command+4).

3. Click to switch to the Audio tab.

4. Choose an option from the Channels menu in the Channel Configuration section of the Audio inspector.

   The choices will vary depending on the source file. For a DSLR workflow, it's very common to switch a Stereo clip to Dual Mono to have better control over the audio channels.

5. Select or deselect the check boxes next to a waveform to mute or unmute an audio channel.

6. You can use the Volume and Pan section to adjust the routing for each channel.

   The Pan Mode preset list offers several easy choices. For dialogue clips, be sure to pan them centered.

▲ The Channel Configuration menu will change based on the available channels in the clip. The most popular choice (that gives the greatest control) is Dual Mono for DSLR footage.

Adjusting Levels

As you combine audio clips, it will often become necessary to adjust their volume. This could be to minimize background sounds and place them under narration or to achieve a consistent volume level for all interviews. This process is essential and one that is frequently revisited while working in an edit.

You can modify the levels of audio for clips in several places:

> Timeline

> Audio inspector

> Modify menu

MODIFY AUDIO IN THE TIMELINE

If a clip appearance setting with audio waveforms is selected in the Timeline, you will also see a purple line for volume control. This horizontal line can be dragged up or down to modify the overall volume of the clip. As you drag, a reading in decibels (dB) is displayed. The drawing for the audio waveform will also update.

Where Timeline adjustments really come in handy is making variable changes in volume. For example, you might want the music to start loudly in the beginning of the video and then gently fade under the first speaker, or you might want the background noise to slowly fade as you transition scenes.

To create this type of fade, you'll use the Range Selection tool:

1. Select a clip in your Timeline.

2. Choose the Range Selection tool (R).

3. Drag in the Timeline to select the area that you want to adjust.

 BREAK APART CLIP ITEMS
Another way to see audio in the Timeline is to select an item and break it apart by pressing Command+Shift+G. This will separate the audio components but leave them connected.

4. Modify the volume within the selected area by dragging up or down.

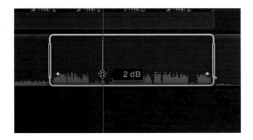

Keyframes are automatically added to create a transition zone between the selected and non-selected areas.

5. You can drag the newly created keyframes left or right to adjust the timing of the fade.

You can use the Inspector for precise control over keyframes.

MODIFY AUDIO IN THE AUDIO INSPECTOR

Whether a clip is selected in the Timeline or in an Event, the Audio inspector can be used. You'll find precise controls for levels, as well as the ability to use automated repairs.

1. Select one or more clips with audio in the Timeline or Event Browser.

2. If it's not visible, open the Audio inspector by clicking the Inspector button in the toolbar and clicking the Audio tab.

3. Use the Volume field or slider to adjust the volume to a desired level.

RESET ALL VOLUME ADJUSTMENTS
If you want to return a clip to its default state, just select a clip in the Timeline or the Event Browser and click the Reset button (a curved arrow).

MODIFY AUDIO IN THE MODIFY MENU

If you learn two keyboard shortcuts, you can also adjust audio directly from your keyboard. If they slip your mind, you'll find useful controls in the Modify menu.

1. Select one or more clips with audio in the Timeline.

2. Choose Modify > Volume and choose Up (Control+=) or Down (Control+-) to modify the volume in 1 or –1 dB increments.

Creating Audio Fades

You already learned how to keyframe audio using the Range Selection tool. There are other ways to quickly add keyframes to fade a clip in or out. These automatic methods will create smoother transitions for your audio clips.

AUTOMATIC CROSSFADES DURING TRANSITIONS

If you add a transition to a video clip that contains audio, Final Cut Pro will automatically add a crossfade transition to the audio. Just use the Transitions tab in the Media Browser to select a video transition, and then drag it onto the clip. Note that this won't work if the audio is detached or expanded from the video.

CROSSFADES

As you learned when trimming in Chapter 8, you can apply a crossfade to the edit point. This will make the transition between two audio clips less abrupt and appear seamless to the viewer's ear. The last thing you want is for a transition to be jarring.

CREATE A FADE USING FADE HANDLES

Another method used with audio is fade handles. These let you drag in the Timeline to create gradual slopes to change volume over time. There are also several presets to make fades easier to apply.

1. Make sure you use an appearance for the Timeline that shows audio detail for your clips.

2. Place the mouse pointer over the top-left or top-right corner of the audio waveform.

3. Fade handles should appear (they look like diamond-shaped keyframes).

4. Move the cursor to position it so you see a double-headed cursor that points left and right.

5. Drag the fade handle to where you want the fade to start or end.

   Fade handles at the beginning of a clip are used to fade in a sound; fade handles at the end will create a fade-out.

6. You can change the shape of the fade by choosing from four presets. Just Control-click a fade handle to see the available options:

   › **Linear.** The Linear option maintains a constant rate of change for the entire length of the fade.

FADES TAKE PRIORITY
A fade created with a fade handle will override a crossfade created by a transition.

▲ The double arrow cursor indicates that a fade handle is available and can be clicked and dragged. The figure on the left shows the cursor change; the figure on the right shows the fade applied.

› **S-curve.** Use this preset to create an ease-in and ease-out.

› **+3dB.** This option begins slowly and then accelerates. This works best when crossfading between two adjacent clips.

› **–3dB.** This preset starts quickly and then slowly tapers off. It is best for quick fades.

Enhancing Audio

When it comes to audio, Final Cut Pro X takes a dual approach to fixing mistakes. You can choose to engage an auto-pilot mode that automatically detects problems and applies recommended fixes. Conversely, an experienced operator can use an extensive collection of audio plug-ins to perform professional restoration. But these approaches aren't exclusive. You can analyze for problems and then manually adjust if you are so inclined.

Analyzing Audio

To fix a clip, you need to know what's "broken." Fortunately, Final Cut Pro X makes this pretty simple. The clip you want to fix needs to be in the Timeline so it can be compared to other clips and evaluated in context. When it comes to fixing the problem, all the controls reside in the Audio Enhancements inspector.

The Audio Enhancements inspector contains three effects:

› **Loudness.** The Loudness effect can be used to make the audio signal a more uniform volume.

› **Background Noise Removal.** This effect looks for unwanted background or low-frequency sounds and then reduces them so your principal audio is clearer.

› **Hum Removal.** If your microphone cables crossed or got too close to a power cord, you may have unwanted hum. This effect reduces common electrical hum noise at either 50 or 60 Hz to deal with the different electric current rates around the world.

Auditioning Music

One of the most useful features in Final Cut Pro X is the ability to audition clips. This feature lets you quickly try out different options as a way to experiment. Although the feature is really designed to let you experiment with different b-roll clips, we think it's great for trying out music options.

Here's how to create an audition in the Event Browser.

1. Select multiple clips that you want to include. Remember that you can hold down the Command key to select multiple items.

2. Choose Clip > Audition > Create (Command+Y).

3. Give the Audition clip a descriptive name.

4. You can then cut the audition into your Timeline. Attach the audio to your primary storyline as you would a standard audio clip.

5. Click the Audition icon in the upper-left corner of the clip to open the Audition window.

6. Turn off skimming by pressing S.

7. Drag your playhead to the starting point of the audition clip.

8. Move the pointer over the Audition window so it is highlighted (make sure skimming is off or this won't work). You also need to make sure the Audition window is active.

9. Press the spacebar to start playback, which will automatically loop.

10. To try another music clip, use the left and right arrow keys to switch clips. When you switch auditioned clips during looped playback, the playhead will jump back to its starting position.

11. When you've decided on the clip you want, click the Done button in the Audition window.

SHOW OR HIDE AUDIO ANIMATION
To show or hide the Audio Animation Editor for the selected clips, press Control+A. This will place each effect or enhancement you've added below the audio clip in the Timeline. You can then expand the clip to see the controls (click the gray arrow at the right edge). You can also use the menu on the clip to see different properties.

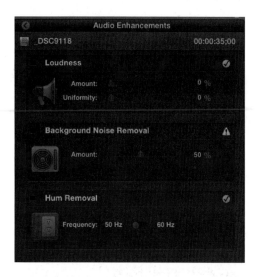

Let's analyze the clips and open the panel.

1. Select a clip in your Timeline (either an audio clip or video clip with audio).

2. Choose Window > Show Audio Enhancements (Command+8).

   When you open the Audio Enhancements inspector, you'll see the gear spinning, which indicates that the clips are being analyzed. You can also track the progress in the Dashboard. If you analyzed clips on import, this step will be skipped.

After the analysis is completed, icons appear next to the three enhancements to show results:

> A red sign indicates severe problems with the clip.

> A yellow warning triangle indicates potential problems that you should listen to.

> A green check mark indicates that the clip is OK.

You can now automatically (or manually) change enhancement settings to correct the problems.

Automatically Enhancing Audio

After you've analyzed a clip, the repair process is pretty simple. Just remember that green is good, yellow means listen carefully, and red means stop and fix it. The automatic enhancements work for loudness, background noise, and hum. Make sure you've analyzed the clip and opened the Audio Enhancements inspector as described in the previous section.

There are a few ways to invoke an auto enhancement. With a clip selected you can:

> Choose Modify > Auto Enhance Audio.

> Choose the Auto Enhance Audio option from the Enhancements menu in the toolbar.

> Click the Auto Enhance button near the bottom of the Audio Enhancements inspector.

THE MEANING OF AUTOMATIC
The automatic enhancements are designed to fix the most common audio problems. These fixes may be truly automatic (perfect the first time) or need minor adjustment of the enhancement's controls.

Recording Narration

Although you're not likely to drag your laptop around as an audio recorder, Final Cut Pro X's ability to record audio directly can be useful. If you connect a USB microphone or use the line-in port, you can easily record voice-over narration.

Here's how to record a narration track.

1. Move the playhead in the Timeline to where you want to start recording.

2. Choose Window > Record Audio.

3. Choose an Event from the Destination menu to store the recording.

4. Use the Input Device menu to change which device is used and how many channels are recorded.

5. Drag the Gain slider to adjust the recording levels of the microphone. Be sure to use the Audio meters to gauge correct audio levels and avoid distortion.

6. Adjust the Monitor settings to avoid feedback. You may need to use headphones or turn off the Monitor altogether (deselect it). Otherwise, you might create a feedback loop of your voice and the speaker, which makes a terrible echo effect.

7. Adjust the output level so you can hear yourself, but not so loud that it affects performance or causes feedback.

8. Click the Record button to start recording.

9. When finished, click the Record button again to stop recording. Your audio recordings are attached to the primary storyline (based on the position of the playhead). They are also stored in the targeted Event.

10. You can record multiple takes by clicking the Record button and repeating steps 8 and 9. Each recording will become a separate connected recording.

When finished, a green check mark appears next to each enhancement that was applied. You'll also see text that offers details about how the clip was fixed. If you want to hear a before and after state, you can select or deselect the blue check box next to each enhancement to toggle it off and on. When finished, you can close the Audio Enhancements inspector by clicking the Back button.

Using Enhancements Manually

If you want to experiment and find the best settings for an enhancement, you can manually adjust the results. Follow the same steps for selecting a clip and opening the Audio Enhancements inspector.

1. Click the icon next to any enhancement with a red or yellow warning (when the enhancement is turned on, its check box is blue).

2. Adjust the properties for each enhancement as needed:

   > **Loudness.** You can drag the Amount percentage slider to increase or decrease the overall loudness (compression) of the clip. You can use the Uniformity slider to increase or decrease the dynamic range of the effect.

   > **Background Noise Removal.** Drag the Amount slider. Be careful about going too far, or you'll add extra distortion to the clip.

   > **Hum Removal.** Select either the 50 Hz or 60 Hz option for Hum Removal.

3. Click the Back button to close the Audio Enhancements inspector.

Adjusting Equalization

Another option in the Audio section is Equalization. Equalization gives you control points for different points in the audio frequency spectrum. You can pull up or down a point to increase or decrease the emphasis of each range. In its simplest form, you may have played with the Bass and Treble on your car stereo or maybe you've opened the 10-band equalizer in iTunes to tweak the sound of your music.

Well, you have the same controls in Final Cut Pro X and more. You can use a 10-band or a 31-band equalizer as well as useful presets. If you don't see these choices, it's probably because you're in the Audio Enhancements inspector (just click the Back button to return to the standard Audio inspector).

Here's how it works.

1. Select a clip you want to modify in the Timeline.

2. Open the Audio inspector and locate the Audio Enhancements section (not the Audio Enhancements inspector).

3. Click the Equalization preset to choose from several standard options.

   Choices like Voice Enhance push the midtones and help a vocal clip really stand out. You can also use the Bass Boost preset to put a little "oomph" into a voice that needs some power.

4. To continue to manually refine the equalization, click the Controls button to make adjustments.

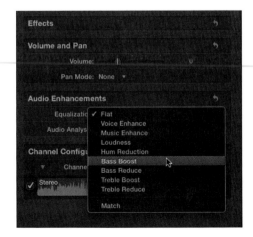

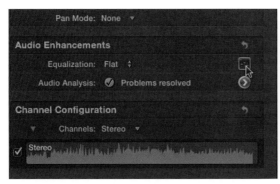
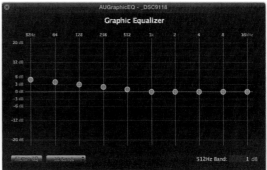

▲ Click the Controls button to open the Graphic Equalizer. The default is a 10-band Equalizer, but you can click the menu in the lower-left corner to switch to 31-bands.

Matching Audio Clips

Another equalization option is Final Cut Pro X's ability to match the sound between multiple clips. This is particularly useful for many audio problems. For example, you may have recorded an interview in two locations. Or perhaps you had multiple cameras covering an Event and the sound is a little different on each camera because the microphones were at different distances. Whatever the cause, the Match Audio function can create a seamless audio mix.

Here's how you can use the Match Audio feature to smooth out the differences between multiple clips.

1. Select one or more clips in the Timeline you want to adjust. Do not include the clip you want to match in the selection.

2. Choose Modify > Match Audio.

   You can also choose Match from the Equalization menu in the Audio Enhancements section of the Audio inspector.

HOW DO I "UN-MATCH" CLIPS?

If you change your mind immediately after a match, you can of course choose Edit > Undo. But if you want to make a change down the road a bit, just click the Equalization menu and choose the Flat setting.

3. Click on the clip you want to use as the target.

   You'll know you've successfully chosen the clip when the Apply Match button at the bottom of the Viewer turns blue.

4. At the bottom of the Viewer, click the Apply Match button.

5. Use the Audio Enhancements section of the Audio inspector to make any additional enhancements you deem necessary.

Additional Audio Effects

If you head on over to the Effects Browser, you'll find several more audio effects to choose from. The effects are organized by category. You'll find Final Cut, Logic, and Apple Audio Unit effects available for several issues. Instead of repeating pages of instruction here, we'll point you to hard-to-find reference guides:

› **For the Logic Effects.** http://manuals.info. apple.com/en_US/final_cut_pro_x_logic_ effects_ref.pdf

› **For the Mac OSX Effects (AU=Audio Units).** http://www.kenstone.net/fcp_homepage/ basic_audio_filter_guide.html

Applying additional effects is easy.

1. Select a clip or multiple clips you want to modify in the Timeline.

2. Click the Effects button in the toolbar to open the Effects Browser.

3. From the Effects Browser, click to choose an audio effect.

   You can preview an audio effect in the currently selected Timeline clip by moving the pointer over the audio effect thumbnails.

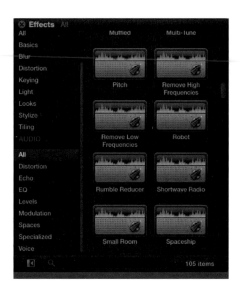

4. Double-click the effect icon to apply it to the selected clip(s).

5. To adjust an effect's properties, switch to the Audio inspector.

6. If the controls aren't visible, click the Show text option next to the Effects section.

7. You can also click the Presets menu to access useful presets.

   Some effects include presets, and all effects support the saving of your own custom settings.

NEED TO FIND AN EFFECT?
To filter which effects are shown in the Effects Browser, just start typing the name of the effect you want into the Effects Browser search field.

KEYFRAMES EQUAL GREATER CONTROL
All effects can use keyframes. By adding distinct points at specific times, you can apply different values to an effect. This can be useful to compensate for variations caused by a moving microphone or subject.

CHAPTER 11

Outputting and Managing Your Project

As you near the end of your project, you'll need to output your video for others. It might be a rough cut to share with your client or others on the team for feedback, or the finished video might be done and ready for the world to see. In any case, Final Cut Pro X offers several options for sharing.

You can easily share with other applications on your Mac, such as iLife, iWork, and Mail. You can also publish for a variety of devices like the iPad or iPhone, or create DVD and Blu-ray Discs. If publishing to the Web is your goal, you'll find quick export to popular sites like YouTube, Facebook, and Vimeo. Final Cut Pro X offers support for numerous other formats, so let's explore your many options.

Sharing Your Project

The Share menu is a standard option in most Apple software. It simplifies the process of exchanging files with other applications and makes the process intuitive with a streamlined output process.

START TO END

The Share menu outputs only a complete project (from beginning to end). If you want to send out only part of a project, you can use Compressor and set In and Out points in its Preview window.

▲ The Share menu offers several options for creating files.

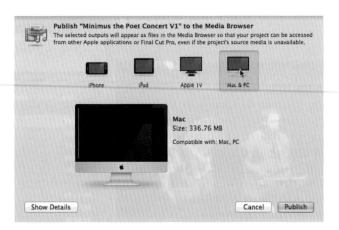

▲ The Mac & PC option offers the highest resolution.

It's important to note that the Share menu will output files as a foreground operation by default. This method produces output faster than others because it takes all resources of the application and devotes them to writing the file (however, you won't be able to do anything else with Final Cut Pro during the output). For many of the share methods, you can choose to have output files created in the background. This means you can keep working on your project in Final Cut Pro as the compression runs in the background.

Sharing with Apple Applications Using the Media Browser

One of the major benefits of Final Cut Pro is how well it works with other Apple software. For example, you can use iLife applications like GarageBand to compose music for your project or iWork applications like Keynote to give a presentation featuring your video project. The Media Browser is accessible in all iLife and iWork applications, and makes your video project available as an asset.

Here's how to send a project to the Media Browser.

1. Select the project (or click in the Timeline) and choose Share > Media Browser.

2. In the next window, select the Apple device that is your primary destination.

    We typically choose Mac & PC for the highest resolution.

3. Click Show Details to output additional sizes and better control the quality of the file.

4. In the Options area, use the controls to determine output:

    › **Sizes.** You can choose one or more sizes. They will be stored as a single entry in the Media Browser.

    › **Encode for.** You can choose "Higher quality" or "More compatibility." As you change options, you'll notice that the file size estimate will update. More important, the list of which devices can play back the file will often update (especially when multiple sizes are chosen). The "Higher quality" options offer the best image clarity but often require the most recent Apple hardware.

> **Compression.** This setting affects the method used to compress the file. The "Better quality (multi-pass)" option will produce the best-looking files but takes longer. It should be reserved for when a project is finished. The "Faster encode (single-pass)" option works well for review copies or if you're in a hurry.

5. Click Advanced to take advantage of Background Rendering. You can perform a background task on your computer or use Compressor (an app that you can purchase separately) to get more options.

6. Click Summary to see precise details about the file(s) that will be generated.

7. Click Publish to share your file to the Media Browser.

    Creating files can take several minutes (especially for a long program). When you click Export, the Share Monitor application opens in your Dock. Just click its icon to check progress. If the icon is bouncing, it means there is a problem with the rendering process. The Share Monitor has its own built-in help system with additional details.

 VERSION CONTROL
Although you could just output a bunch of files, the Media Browser always makes the latest version available to iLife and iWork applications. Whenever you make changes in Final Cut Pro, the Media Browser can be updated.

WHERE'S MY MEDIA?
If you open an iLife or iWork application, just click Media (or choose View > Show Media Browser) to open the Media Browser. You'll find any shared Final Cut Pro X project in the Movies area.

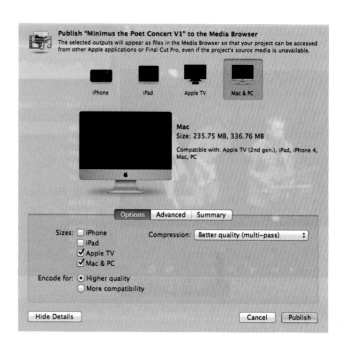

▲ The Encode for and Compression options will produce great variations in file size and compatibility. Be sure to examine both options carefully.

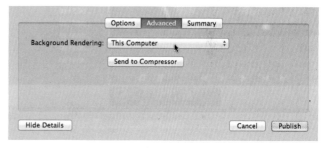

▲ You can use Background Rendering or Compressor to create files in the background.

Transferring to Apple Devices with iTunes

Another great way to share your video project is with the wide range of Apple devices. You can take your video to go using iTunes and an iPhone, iPad, or iPod. You can also stream a video to a high-definition television using an Apple TV.

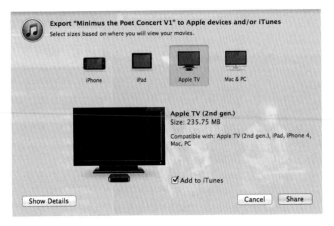

▲ Clicking the Show Details button allows you to choose multiple output sizes.

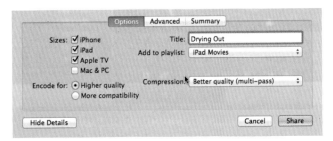

▲ The multi-pass compression option is best for final output of a completed project.

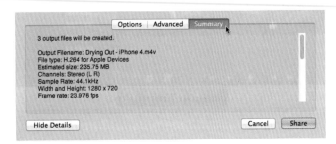

▲ The summary tab should be reviewed before clicking the Share button.

Here's how to send your project to iTunes.

1. Select the project (or click in the Timeline) and choose Share > Apple Devices.

2. In the next window, select the Apple device that is your primary destination.

3. Make sure the Add to iTunes option is selected to put the file directly in your iTunes library.

4. Click Show Details to output additional sizes and better control the quality of the file.

5. In the Options area, use the controls to determine output:

    > **Sizes.** You can choose one or more sizes to send to iTunes. If you have multiple Apple devices, be sure to choose them here.

    > **Encode for.** These options are identical to those you used in the Media Browser. Be sure that changing an encoding method does not mean your targeted device becomes unsupported.

    > **Title.** Give the movie a descriptive title. You can also add delineations like rough cut or approval copy to help with version control.

    > **Add to playlist.** Any existing playlists in iTunes can be chosen. This can help control syncing or library organization.

    > **Compression.** This setting affects the method used to compress the file. We recommend the slower but significantly clearer "Better quality (multi-pass)" option.

6. Click Advanced to take advantage of Background Rendering.

7. Click Summary to see precise details about the file(s) that will be generated.

8. Click Share to send your file(s) to iTunes on your computer.

    As before, rendering files can take several minutes (especially for a long program). Use the Share Monitor application (in your Dock) to track progress.

9. When the sharing process is complete, iTunes will open. You can then view the movie on your computer, stream it to an Apple TV, or transfer it to a synced device.

Sending a Video with Apple Mail

You can easily attach a movie file to an email to send to a team member or client. Due to the limitations of email (a ban on large attachments for most), we have a very specific workflow.

1. Select the project (or click in the Timeline) and choose Share > Email.

2. Using the Frame Size menu, choose a targeted size. We recommend using the Small option (especially if your program is long). Many servers are set to reject large attachments.

3. Choose an encoding method using the Compression menu. The best option to use is "Better quality (multi-pass)" because it results in a smaller file size (but does take longer).

4. Click Advanced to take advantage of Background Rendering.

5. Click Summary to see precise details about the file(s) that will be generated.

6. Click Compose Message to send your file.

   Mail opens and a new email with the movie attached is created. We highly recommend sending another message (without an attachment) to alert the receiver to look for the large file and other message and to confirm receipt.

Posting a Video on the Web

Final Cut Pro offers the ability to post your video to different video sharing sites. This lets you post your movie for others to view online without having to email large files. These sharing sites also work well with streaming video to devices, which can help you extend the reach of your video. The three most useful services we use are Vimeo, Facebook, and YouTube.

▲ With iTunes and AirPlay, you can stream your videos to an Apple TV.

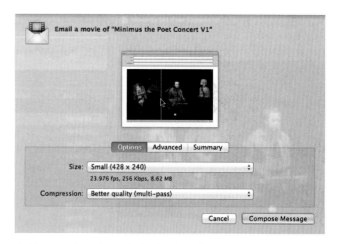

▲ You can drag through the preview thumbnail to update and preview your video.

 READ THE TERMS OF SERVICE
By posting a video to a sharing site, you are granting that site certain rights to redistribute (and even monetize on their behalf) your content. Be sure to closely read the terms of service for each site before posting. Final Cut Pro will show you a link to the terms in the Share window. In our opinion, Vimeo has the most artist-friendly terms that protect the original copyright holders' rights the most.

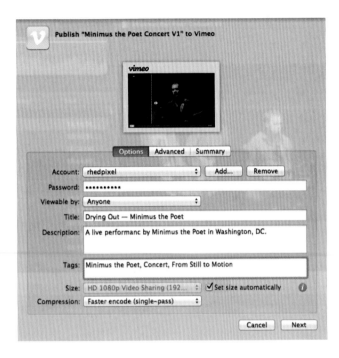

VIMEO

Vimeo is a popular website for sharing video (especially among professional and amateur filmmakers). It offers both free and paid accounts with different levels of service. Once you've set up a Vimeo account, you publish a project to Vimeo directly from Final Cut Pro.

1. Select the project (or click in the Timeline) and choose Share > Vimeo.

2. Choose an account from the Account menu, or click Add to add an existing account.

   You can add more than one account to the list but can only export to one at a time.

3. Fill in the requests field:

   › **Password.** Enter your Vimeo account password. For security purposes, you'll need to enter it each time you want to publish.

   › **Viewable by.** Choose who can see the video.

   › **Title.** Enter a name for the movie so others can search for it.

   › **Description.** The information here helps power search features on the site and can convince others to watch your movie.

   › **Tags.** You can use keywords to help viewers find your movie.

4. Select the "Set size automatically" option or deselect it and choose from the menu to control the size of the output movie.

   Vimeo has limits on free accounts as to how many clips and data can be uploaded each week.

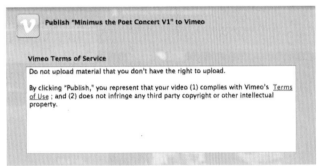

▲ Click the blue hypertext to go directly to the terms of service and review the rights you are granting the video hosting provider.

5. Use the Compression menu as well as the Advanced and Summary areas to control the quality of the file generated. These controls are identical to the options previously discussed.

6. Click Next to read the terms of service.

7. When ready, click Publish.

   You can monitor progress with the Share Monitor in your Dock.

ANOTHER EMAIL?

If you've used the Share menu to post a movie to a service like YouTube, Vimeo, or Facebook, you can send a message from the Sharing inspector. Just click the menu next to a sharing option and choose Tell a Friend.

FACEBOOK

Facebook is a very popular social networking site. In fact, in many countries, more than 50 percent of all adults have an account. Facebook is a free service that makes it easy to share video and news with friends, family, and colleagues.

Once you've set up a Facebook account, you publish a project to Facebook directly from Final Cut Pro.

1. Select the project (or click in the Timeline) and choose Share > Facebook.

2. Choose an account from the Account menu, or click Add to add an existing account.

▶ To add a new account, click the Add button. You'll need the email address used for your profile page and your login password to connect Final Cut Pro to the social media site.

Controlling Shared Projects

Once you've published a project using any of the share options, the Share icon is added next to the project name in the Timeline and Project Library. This is an easy way to tell which projects are being shared as well as control them.

1. Click a Share icon in the Project Library to open the Sharing inspector.

2. Examine the Sharing inspector to see when the project was published and to which other applications or devices.

3. Click the menu next to a share method to access additional controls for share options (most support extra options).

4. You can also click Properties to see details about referenced Events as well as to view or add any notes about the project.

As you continue to work with a project, you may notice an exclamation mark next to the Share icon, which warns you that a project has changed since you last shared it. Be sure to repeat the Share command for any formats you want to update.

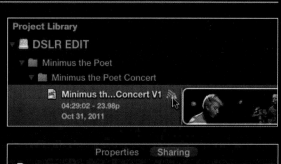

3. Fill in the requests field:

> **Password.** Enter your Facebook account password. For security purposes, you'll need to enter it each time you want to publish.

> **Viewable by.** Choose who can see the video. You can limit viewers to your Friends or Friends of Friends. You can also set the video to Everyone to make it completely public and gain the largest audience.

> **Title.** Enter a name for the movie so others can search for it.

> **Description.** The information here helps power search features on the site and can convince others to watch your movie.

4. Select the "Set size automatically" option or deselect it and choose from the menu to control the size of the output movie.

5. Use the Compression menu as well as the Advanced and Summary areas to control the quality of the file generated. These controls are identical to the options previously discussed.

6. Click Next to read the terms of service.

7. When ready, click Publish.

You can monitor progress with the Share Monitor in your Dock.

YOUTUBE

YouTube is the world's most popular site dedicated to sharing video online. All accounts are free and produce video files that are compatible with many different devices.

Once you've set up a YouTube account, you publish a project to YouTube directly from Final Cut Pro.

1. Select the project (or click in the Timeline) and choose Share > YouTube.

2. Choose an account from the Account menu, or click Add to add an existing account.

3. Fill in the requests field:

> **Password.** Enter your YouTube account password. For security purposes, you'll need to enter it each time you want to publish.

> **Category.** YouTube offers several categories to help organize its large collection of movies.

> **Title.** Enter a name for the movie so others can search for it.

> **Description.** The information here helps power search features on the site and can convince others to watch your movie.

> **Tags.** You can use keywords to help viewers find your movie.

4. Deselect the "Make this movie private" option to allow the most folks to see your movie or use the privacy options to specify contacts in your YouTube account settings.

 WHAT ABOUT OTHER WEBSITES?
You can always export a movie by choosing Share > Export Media. This movie can then be posted to other sites. You'll need to manually do this process as well as upload project metadata.

5. Select the "Set size automatically" option or deselect it and choose from the menu to control the size of the output movie.

6. Use the Compression menu as well as the Advanced and Summary areas to control the quality of the file generated. These controls are identical to the options previously discussed.

7. Click Next to read the terms of service.

8. When ready, click Publish.

   You can monitor progress with the Share Monitor in your Dock.

Burning to Disc

An easy way to share your movie with others (especially those without computers or portable media players) is to burn a movie to an optical disc. With Final Cut Pro, you can create a standard-definition DVD or a Blu-ray–compatible disc.

NEED HARDWARE?
Although most Macs come with a SuperDrive that can burn DVDs (the MacBook Air does not, but it can be purchased separately), you'll need to invest if you want to make Blu-ray discs. Many manufacturers make Mac-compatible external optical drives that support Blu-ray burning to blue laser media. If your computer lacks a drive, you can also create a disk image (.img) file. This can be copied to another computer with a burner and turned into a playable disc with Disk Utility.

DVD

A standard DVD will work in both a DVD player connected to a television and many computers with a DVD drive. Your video will only display in standard definition (even if you shot in HD). The DVD format is broadly compatible and very affordable.

1. Select the project (or click in the Timeline) and choose Share > DVD.

2. Choose an output device. You can use a connected disc burner or choose Hard Drive to make an image file.

3. Specify an option from the Layers menu.

   The Automatic option works well if you have the DVD media already loaded. This ensures that you can write the highest quality file.

4. Choose a template from the "Disc template" menu.

   These basic themes can be slightly customized.

5. Enter a name for the menu in the Title field.

6. Choose an option from the "When disc loads" menu.

   You can have a menu appear or have the movie start playing immediately.

7. Click the Add button and choose a graphic file to create a menu background.

   You can use an application like Keynote or Adobe Photoshop to create the menu page background.

8. Use the Advanced and Summary areas to control the quality of the file generated. These controls are identical to the options previously discussed.

9. When ready, make sure a blank disk is inserted and click Burn.

10. Follow any onscreen prompts.

FANCIER DVDS

If you want more control over DVD options, you can use iDVD or DVD Studio Pro. Both applications were sold previously in bundles of iLife and Final Cut Studio (and may already be installed from earlier versions). Just export a media file at full quality and import the clip to use.

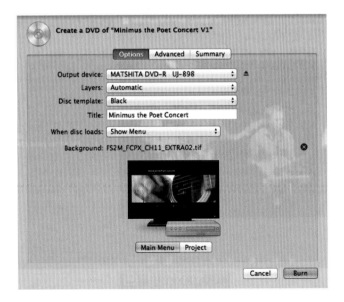

Blu-ray Discs

If you'd like to publish your movie for playback on a High Definition television, a Blu-ray disc may be the right choice. These discs will work on dedicated players as well as popular gaming systems like the Sony PlayStation 3.

To create a true Blu-ray disc, you may need to purchase a special burner because a standard Mac SuperDrive cannot use this format. You may be able to use the standard Mac SuperDrive to create an AVCHD disc that works on many players.

1. Select the project (or click in the Timeline) and choose Share > Blu-ray.

2. Choose an output device. You can use a connected disc burner or choose Hard Drive to make an image file.

3. Specify an option from the Layers menu.

   The Automatic option is best, but you must have the optical media already loaded.

4. Choose a template from the "Disc template" menu.

   These basic themes can be slightly customized.

5. Enter a name for the menu in the Title field.

6. Choose an option from the "When disc loads" menu.

   You can have a menu appear or have the movie start playing immediately. You may also be able to select the "Include loop movie button" on some templates to create a continuously looping movie. Be sure your project has fades at the front and back for a smoother transition

7. Click any of the Add buttons to customize the appearance of the menu:

   › **Background.** A full-screen graphic (sized 1280x720 or 1920x1080 pixels) can be used to create a themed background.

> **Logo graphic.** A logo for the client or project can be used. A PNG or PSD file with transparency works best. The logo will be placed in the upper-right corner and is reduced in size.

> **Title graphic.** You can create a fancier title graphic using an image-editing program. A PNG or PSD file with transparency works best. The title is the largest element and is centered on the screen.

8. Use the Advanced and Summary areas to control the quality of the file generated. These controls are identical to the options previously discussed.

9. When ready, make sure a blank disk is inserted and click Burn.

10. Follow any onscreen prompts.

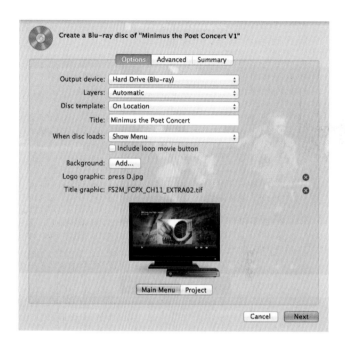

NEED TO SKIP FORWARD?
Final Cut Pro automatically adds a marker every 30 seconds in a project. Markers let you use a remote to skip forward or backward 30 seconds each time the Next Chapter or Previous Chapter button is pressed. If you want to manually set chapter markers, you'll need to use the Send to Compressor option (and have Compressor installed). This will let you add and name chapter markers using its Preview window.

Exporting Your Project

Final Cut Pro easily integrates with several applications, devices, and services, but there are still more options. If you need to send movie files to another application that's not supported by the workflows already discussed, you can create a master file or specific compression for sharing.

Exporting a Movie File

Here's how to create a self-contained QuickTime movie of your project.

1. Select the project (or click in the Timeline) and choose Share > Export Media (Command+E).

   A new panel opens with several options.

2. From the Export menu, choose what you'd like to create.

   You can easily save a standard movie with the Video and Audio option, or create Video Only or Audio Only. Additionally, if you've assigned specific roles to audio or video files, you can create separate audio and video tracks or output files. (Be sure to see the online help for more on roles if you need dedicated stem export.)

3. Choose a setting from the "Video codec" menu.

   The Current Settings option will make a master file that matches the project's properties. You can also choose one of the available codecs and presets, such as Apple ProRes, H.264, DVCPRO HD, HDV, or XDCAM.

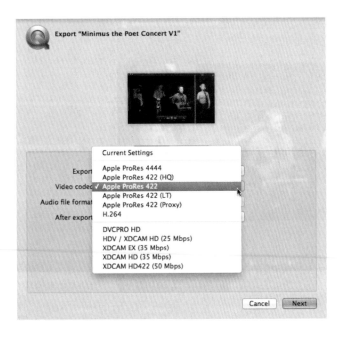

4. Specify what to do with the exported file from the "After export" menu.

   › **Do Nothing.** An output file is written to disk.

   › **Open with QuickTime Player.** The new file opens in QuickTime Player so that you can review it for data integrity.

   › **Open with Compressor.** The new file is sent to Compressor where it serves as the source file for a new batch. This is a great work-flow to create a less compressed master file with one of the Apple ProRes presets that can also produce several derivative compressions. This option is available only if Compressor is installed on the same computer as Final Cut Pro.

5. Click the Summary area to review the quality of the file to be generated.

6. Click Next.

7. Enter a filename and choose a location for the exported file.

8. Click Save.

   Final Cut Pro renders and saves your movie to the targeted directory. A window appears to show the render progress.

Exporting a Still Image

You can easily save a single frame of video as a still image. This new file will contain any effects or changes you made in the Timeline and is essentially a "freeze frame." This is a useful output option when making files for use on websites or as small prints. They can also be used as specific thumbnail images by many video websites.

1. Position the playhead in your Timeline on the frame you want to save.

2. Choose Share > Save Current Frame.

3. Choose a format from the Export menu.

▲ You can only export one still image format at a time.

EXPORTING AN AUDIO-ONLY FILE
You may want to send out just an audio file. It might be a transcript that you'd like to create to put on a web page or help with editing. Or maybe it's the audio from a long concert. Simply choose Audio Only from the Export menu. You can choose to create an AAC, AC3, AIFF, CAF, MP3, or WAVE file.

WHICH FILE FORMAT?
Although you can target some high-end image formats like DPX, IFF, or OpenEXR for advanced digital cinema workflows, the more common JPEG, Photoshop, PNG, or TIFF formats are likely the more useful choices.

4. Click the Summary area to review the quality of the file to be generated.

5. Click Next.

6. Enter a filename and choose a location for the exported file.

7. Click Save.

Exporting with Compressor

Earlier in this chapter you learned about Apple Compressor, a dedicated compression utility available from the Mac App Store. If you have this application installed, several additional controls become available. Many of the share methods feature a Send to Compressor button in the output controls that can jump-start a compression project by transferring essential settings. The following sections explain a few other ways to access Compressor as well.

SEND TO COMPRESSOR

You can send an entire project to Compressor so that you can export using its customized export settings. You can also set In and Out points in Compressor to use only part of a project.

1. Select the project (or click in the Timeline) and choose Share > Send to Compressor.

Apple Compressor opens and your project transfers.

2. In the Preview window you can set In and Out points to define a range for the project.

3. Choose one or more settings from the Settings area and drag it onto the job.

4. Drag a destination from the Destinations tab onto the job to specify where the file should be stored.

5. When ready, click Submit.

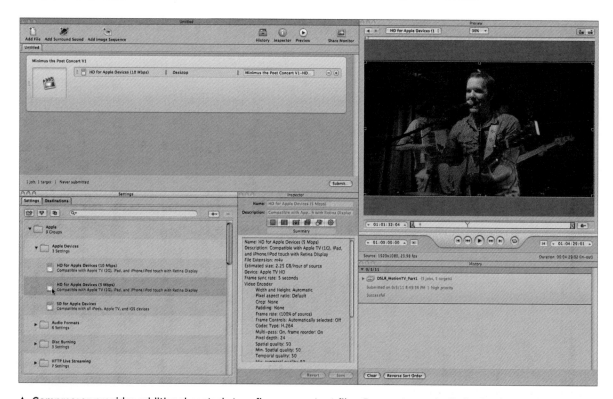

▲ Compressor provides additional controls to refine your output files. Be sure to use both the Settings and Destinations tabs to define your formats and outputs.

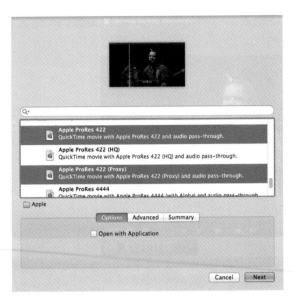

▲ Hold down the Command key when clicking if you want to choose multiple files. You can also use the search field to narrow your choices.

EXPORT USING COMPRESSOR SETTINGS

If you want to use the installed Compressor settings or custom settings you've created, you can choose a single or even multiple settings for output from within a single dialog.

1. Select the project (or click in the Timeline) and choose Share > Export Using Compressor Settings.

2. In the new window that opens, choose one or more settings.

3. Use the Advanced and Summary areas to control the quality of the file generated. These controls are identical to the options previously discussed.

4. Click the Next button.

5. Enter a base filename and choose a location for the exported file.

6. Click Save.

Exporting a Master File

When a project is done, you'll likely think of all sorts of places it can go. Sure, the Web, your iPad, and even a Blu-ray disc are all excellent ways to distribute your movie, but they aren't future proof.

Professional editors always back up their final project as a self-contained movie file using the least compression possible. This ensures that a large file is written that preserves the color and audio details. It also gives you a high-quality backup that can be recompressed and delivered again in the future. This helps ensure against data loss and is often faster than reconnecting and rerendering an entire project.

Here's how to make a master file.

1. Select the project (or click in the Timeline) and choose Share > Export Media (Command+E). A new panel opens with several options.

2. From the Export menu, choose the Video and Audio option.

3. From the "Video codec" menu, choose the Apple ProRes 422 (HQ) option for a DSLR project. If you've mixed in higher bit rate footage, you can consider the ProRes 4444 option.

4. Click Next, enter a filename, and choose a location for the exported file.

5. Click Save.

6. Back up the file to multiple locations and use at least two different types of storage media to keep it safe.

Managing Projects and Media

As your project comes to a close, you'll want to be sure to back up your assets and project files. Final Cut Pro offers several options for media management. Some techniques can be done in Final Cut Pro, and others require working in Final Cut Pro and the Finder.

How Files Are Stored

When you first create a new Event or project, files and folders are created on your hard drive. These folders are precisely set up and need to be backed up in their entirety to successfully preserve data. Files are created differently, depending on the original location selected:

› **Local drive.** If an Event or project is on your local system, you'll find its folders in your Movies folder in your User home folder (/Users/user-name/Movies/). This is the default location for your Final Cut Pro files.

› **External drive.** If you targeted an external drive for an Event or project, you'll find its folders are at the main, or root, level of your device.

› **Storage Area Network (SAN).** If you are using a storage device connected to a local network, your Event or project can be in any folder you've added.

EVENT FILES

When you create a new Event, a folder and subfolder structure is set up. The contents of the Event folder depends on the options you selected in the Import preferences:

› **Analysis Files.** This folder contains the analysis files that are used and managed by Final Cut Pro. These help with tasks like stabilization, rolling shutter, and color balance. Do not move, modify, or delete this folder.

› **Original Media.** This folder contains either the original files imported from your camera or an alias file that points to the original files.

› **Render Files.** This folder holds render files related to your media. Do not move, modify, or delete this folder.

› **Transcoded Media.** If you've used the create optimized or proxy media options, the generated media is located in this folder.

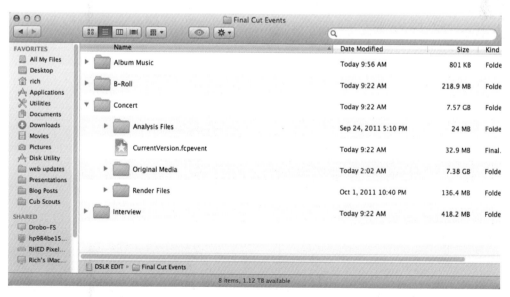

▲ Final Cut Events will contain multiple folders and files. You need all of the folders inside an Event to make a complete and working Event.

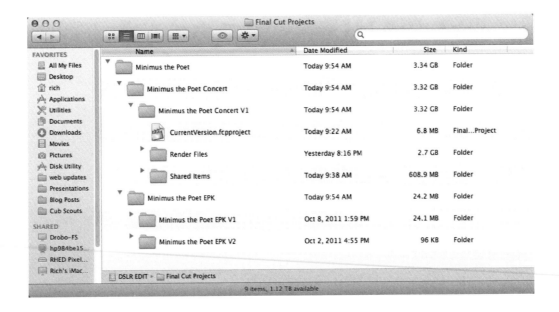

PROJECT FILES

When you set up a new project, Final Cut Pro creates a new folder to hold essential details. When backing up or copying a project file, you'll need all of these items:

> **Project file.** A Final Cut Pro project file has an .fcpproject extension. The project file should not be moved, modified, or deleted.

> **Render Files.** This folder holds render files related to your project. Do not move, modify, or delete this folder.

Deleting Render Files

As you work with a project, render files can start to pile up. For example, you might experiment with different looks for your footage or try out different animated titles. Over time, files can accumulate and take up disk space.

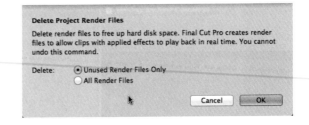

BACKING UP IN THE FINDER
You can back up an Event or project by simply copying it to an external drive. These backups can be accessed through the Event or Project Library and can even be moved to a different machine.

Final Cut Pro makes it easy to delete unused render files for both projects and Events.

DELETE PROJECT RENDER FILES

A project's render files are stored in the project folder. Do not access these from the Finder; rather, use a dedicated Final Cut Pro command.

1. Select a project in the Project Library.

2. Choose File > Delete Project Render Files.

   A new window appears.

Delete Project Render Files

Delete render files to free up hard disk space. Final Cut Pro creates render files to allow clips with applied effects to play back in real time. You cannot undo this command.

Delete: ⦿ Unused Render Files Only
          ◯ All Render Files

                                    Cancel   OK

---

3. Choose to delete Unused Render Files Only.

4. Click OK to purge the files.

DELETE EVENT RENDER FILES

Render files associated with your media are stored in the Event folder. Just like project render files, you'll want to work through Final Cut Pro for cleanup.

1. Select an Event in the Event Browser.

2. Choose File > Delete Event Render Files.

   A new window appears.

3. Choose to delete Unused Render Files Only.

4. Click OK to purge the files.

Moving (or Duplicating) a Project and Media Files

If you'd like to bring a project to another system, it's pretty easy. Final Cut Pro can move or duplicate a project to a new drive. Move is the best choice to relocate a project; duplicate makes a second copy to the targeted drive.

1. Make sure that a project is open and that all referenced media is online and available.

   If you have offline media, be sure to see the article "Solutions to common media management issues" in the Help Center.

2. Switch to the Project Library and select the desired project.

3. Choose one of these options:

   > File > Move Project to copy the file to another location and then delete it from its original location

   > File > Duplicate Project to create a second copy of a project and its related assets

   With either option, a new window opens. The choices will vary slightly.

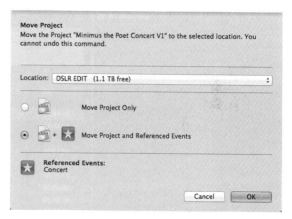

▲ When you move a project, you can choose to bring any referenced events with it.

▲ The Duplicate Project + Used Clips Only option is a useful way to back up only what was used in a project.

4. Choose an external storage device or an internal drive from the Location menu.

5. Choose from the following options:

> When moving a project, you can choose to just move the project file. This is useful to relocate the project from one drive to another. If you want the media to also travel, select the Move Project and Referenced Events option to move the project file and any Events (with media).

> When duplicating a project, you can just create a second copy of the project file. If you want all of the media to travel (including unused footage), select the Duplicate Project and Referenced Events option. If you want to take only footage that appears in a project, select the Duplicate Project + Used Clips Only option. With this last option, be sure to enter a descriptive name in the New Event Name field.

6. Click OK to create the copy or move.

Be sure to attach the storage to a second computer or unmount your current drives except for the new hard drive to check if the copy was successful. Do this before you erase any projects or media. Also, quit Final Cut Pro before detaching any hard drives because they may be in use.

▲ Consolidating a project is useful if it is going to be spread over multiple drives.

Consolidating a Project and Media

As you build your project, it's possible that media files will get spread out over several locations. For example, you might have video footage on a dedicated drive but music and photos from your internal iPhoto and iTunes libraries. Before running the consolidate option, you may want to move a project file using the method described in the previous section.

Here's how to consolidate media for a project.

1. Select a project you want to consolidate in the Project Library.

2. Control-click on the project and choose Consolidate Project Media.

If a window appears stating that there is nothing to consolidate, your media files are already consolidated to one disk.

3. Choose *one* of the following options to consolidate the files:

> **Copy Referenced Events.** Duplicates the referenced Events (and all the clips in those Events) to the location of your project. You may want to select this option if you use the same media in multiple projects or if you haven't finished adding clips from the Event to your project.

> **Move Referenced Events.** Moves all the referenced Events to the location of your project. If there are other projects that use the clips in the Event you're consolidating, those projects may not have access to the Event (and you may need to update the project's Referenced Events in the Inspector). You may want to select this option if the clips in the Event are only used in the project you're consolidating.

> **Copy Used Clips Only.** Duplicates only those media files used in the project (not all the clips in the Events referenced by the project). This is a good option to use if you want to conserve disk space. Be sure to enter a name in the New Event Name field if you're using this option.

4. Click OK to start the consolidation.

Final Cut Pro consolidates the project's media using the method you selected. The Event or Events appear on the same hard drive as the project file.

Where to Now?

Welcome to the start of your journey. With the essential skills we've covered in this book, you should be able to edit your projects and solve common production problems. Of course, when it comes to video editing, the journey never really ends. Here are a few additional ways to stay in touch with the authors and learn more about DSLR video production and editing:

> **From Still to Motion Facebook Page.** Be sure to become a fan of the official From Still to Motion page at facebook.com/DSLRVideo for regular updates of news and information.

> **Creative COW Forums.** You'll find news, forums, and podcasts at www.CreativeCOW.net. Richard Harrington and Robbie Carmen can both be reached this way.

> **Lynda.com.** If you're looking for additional video-based training, Abba Shapiro and Robbie Carman have titles available through this website.

> **RichardHarringtonBlog.com.** Rich maintains an extensive personal blog with daily updates on all things photography and video.

> **Twitter.** If you'd like to keep up-to-date on the authors' activities, you can follow @rhedpixel, @abbashapiro, and @robbiecarman.

Index

stabilization, analyzing video for, 26
stereo audio, grouping, 27
stereo channel, configuring, 145
still images. *See also* photos
    adding to projects, 92
    default duration, 92
    exporting, 168–169
    recompressing, 26
storage area network (SAN), using, 61
stories, enhancing, 78
storyline, primary, 83, 88
sync command, troubleshooting, 68
sync point, finding, 70
synced footage, creating Smart
  Collections of, 74. *See also* footage
Synchronize Clips keyboard shortcut,
  68–69, 71
syncing footage
    clips automatically, 67–68
    interviews automatically, 70–71
    with markers, 69
    multiple cameras, 71–73
    turning off bad tracks, 73
    using best audio, 73

T

Tascam audio recorders, 9
timecode. *See also* drop frame
  timecode
    changing, 59
    displaying for clips, 80
    setting, 58
timecode value, entering to move
  clips, 88
Timeline
    adding clips to, 82–85
    adjusting settings, 91
    arranging clips in, 86–90
    deleting clips from, 99–100
    deleting ranges from, 99–100
    displaying audio waveforms in,
     141
    dragging to, 58
    holding space in, 84–85
    mixing formats in, 131–133
    modifying audio in, 146–147
    moving clips in, 107–108
    navigation techniques, 91
    removing clips from, 82–85
    scrolling in, 90
    selecting ranges in, 82
    zooming in, 87, 90
Timeline Index
    navigating Timeline with, 92–93
    reassigning roles in, 44
    viewing roles in, 44

Titles role, 42, 44
transcoding
    Apple ProRes options, 35
    considering, 25
    optimized media, 25, 35
    options, 35
    proxy media, 25
transferring media
    card reader, 17
    computer selection, 15–16
    connectivity, 16
    creating disk images, 18–19
    offloading cards, 17–18
    portable drive, 16
    software, 16
transitions
    adding, 110–113
    audio crossfade, 113
    Available Media setting, 111
    changing, 112
    copying to edit points, 113
    cross dissolve, 112
    customizing, 112
    Default Duration setting, 111
    deleting, 113
    detaching audio, 113
    Full Overlap setting, 111
    impact on show pacing, 111
    listing, 113
    overlap and handles, 111
    preference settings, 111
    video-only, 113
Transitions Browser, using, 112
trash
    emptying, 53
    moving projects to, 63
Trim tool
    Roll edit points with, 103
    switching to, 103
trimming edits, 101–108. *See also*
  advanced editing commands; edits
    Ripple edit tool, 102–103
    Roll edit, 103–104
    Slide edit, 107–108
    Slip edit, 106–107
trimming feedback, showing details of,
  105

U

UDMA memory cards, 15

V

Van Hurkman, Alexis, 126
Vectorscope, using, 120
video

adding only, 99
analyzing, 26
collapsing, 142
cutting sound bites, 78
deciding on starting point, 78
detaching audio from, 142
formats, 6
posting on Web, 161–165
sending with Apple Mail, 161
showing expanded, 142
syncing with audio, 67–73
video properties, deleting, 59
video quality, choosing, 35
Video role, 42, 44
video scopes. *See* scopes
video-based training, resource for,
  175
video-only transition, adding, 113
Vimeo, publishing projects to, 162

W

Waveform Monitor, using, 120
waveforms
    displaying, 142
    displaying in Timeline, 141
    enabling subframe viewing, 143
    turning on second set of, 141
    viewing in greater details, 143
websites
    Creative COW Forums, 175
    Lynda.com, 175
    RichardHarringtonBlog.com, 175
    From Still to Motion, 175
    Twitter, 175

Y

YouTube, publishing projects to,
  164–165

Z

Zoom audio recorders, 9
zooming in Timeline, 69, 87, 90